GROWING UP IN THE FORTIES

Grace Horseman

ISIS
LARGE PRINT
Oxford, England

First published in Great Britain 1997
by Constable and Company Limited

Published in Large Print 1998 by ISIS Publishing Ltd,
7 Centremead, Osney Mead, Oxford OX2 0ES,
by arrangement with Constable and Company Limited

British Library Cataloguing in Publication Data
Growing up in the forties. – Large print ed. –
(Reminiscence series)
1. Large type books 2. Great Britain – Social life and customs
– 20th century 3. Great Britain – Social conditions –
20th century
I. Horseman, Grace
941'.084'0922

ISBN 0-7531-5060-3

Printed and bound by MPG Books Ltd, Bodmin, Cornwall

CONTENTS

PREFACE

This is the fourth book in the living history series, covering the first half of the 20th century. Together they span the years from the cart-and-horse, dustpan-and-brush era to the discovery of radio, television, motor cars, aeroplanes and much more.

Each contributor has his or her own recollections of life as it was in the decade. Naturally the Forties are dominated by the Second World War, but there is also much about the lighter side of life in that period.

"The Little Salamander" by Walter de la Mare is reproduced by kind permission of the Literary Trustees of Walter de la Mare, and the Society of Authors as their representative.

INTRODUCTION

The "Threadbare Thirties" ended with the outbreak of the Second World War, followed by the ferocious Forties. By January 1940 the phoney war was well established but any feelings of complacency were soon shattered. Norway, Denmark, Holland and Belgium were each invaded by Germany, and then it was the turn of France. Victory was almost in Hitler's grasp but the miraculous evacuation of the British and other troops from Dunkirk changed the face of the war.

Chamberlain gave way to Winston Churchill, who headed a National Government. Among ministers, Lord Woolton was outstanding as Minister of Food, doing much to make rationing fair and the diet wholesome, if sparse. Churchill said he had nothing to offer but blood, toil, tears and sweat, but his speeches inspired new determination among civilians and troops alike. The Battle of Britain followed, when the few Royal Air Force pilots were pitted against massed German bomber attacks on airfields, London and other cities. They were victorious, but at great cost.

When the Japanese bombed Pearl Harbour without warning in December 1941, sinking part of the American Pacific fleet, America was finally drawn into the war. Britain (with loyal support from the Dominions) no longer stood alone.

War, with its rationing, bombing and the evacuation of

children and families, was to dominate life in Britain during the first half of the Forties. When atomic bombs were dropped on Japan in August 1945 the war was brought to an abrupt end. Once peace was declared there was a slow return to normality, but some scars would never be healed.

However, many people looked back on their war years as a time of close companionship, when many class barriers were broken down. Sharing communal shelters and neighbours helping one another created a completely new atmosphere. In the Forces, too, barriers were broken down as men of very different backgrounds lived and shared danger together.

Radio was an important part of life. Not only did listeners rely on it for the latest news, but it also provided the entertainment that was so necessary under the stress of war. It was also used to send coded messages to Resistance fighters on the Continent. The Forties was the time of the big bands and dancing; cinemas and theatres flourished, with people queuing for seats in spite of the risk of air-raids. The trend continued after the war.

War-weary Britons were longing for a change, so when Churchill called an election in 1945 there was a landslide victory for Labour. Clement Attlee became Prime Minister, Ernest Bevin was moved to the Foreign Office, and his place at the Ministry of Labour was taken by George Isaacs. Sir Stafford Cripps became President of the Board of Trade and Hugh Dalton Chancellor of the Exchequeur. Many of the policies they carried out had been prepared by the Coalition Government: the 1944 Education Act of R. A. Butler, and the Beveridge Report that was to find fulfilment in the formation in 1948 of the new National Health Service. Unemployment benefit and Old Age pensions were introduced and for the first time there was a burial allowance.

With so much destruction during the war, housing was a major problem. Materials were in short supply and many of the skilled workers had yet to be discharged from the services. Those who had come out of retirement left the jobs they had undertaken during the war, adding to the shortfall. The problem of unlimited growth in suburban London was recognised, so the New Towns act of 1946 provided for the creation of 15 new towns. Although only 55,000 houses were completed in 1946 that number increased to around 200,000 annually.

When the war ended the length of compulsory schooling was extended to the age of 15. Direct-grant grammar schools received assistance directly from the government, on condition that at least 25 per cent of their pupils held free places paid for by the local authorities. The remaining secondary schools were grouped into grammar, secondary modern and technical, and pupils were allocated according to their ability, as shown by results in an examination at 11-plus. University education was made free for everyone who had the ability to profit from it.

From its early days Labour had believed in the public ownership of production, distribution and exchange. The Bank of England was the first institution to be nationalised in 1946, and in 1947 the National Coal Board came into being. Later that year the railways, the canals, Port Authorities and London Transport were nationalised.

Britain emerged from the war much impoverished and

also with the perceived threat of Communist Russia and the Cold War that was to follow. India was granted independence in 1947 and the new state of Pakistan was created. In 1948 the State of Israel was created, and in 1949 Eire became the Republic of Ireland, no longer part of the Commonwealth. With the reallocation of land on the Continent, the map of the world was changing, but everywhere there was a yearning for peace.

CHAPTER ONE

Family Life

By the end of the Thirties Great Britain was already in a state of war. Children had been evacuated to the comparative safety of the country, but as the phoney war continued, many parents decided that their offspring should return home. However, once air-raids on London and elsewhere became acute later in 1940, some of these were re-evacuated and some were sent abroad.

For many children this experience was to change their lives, but it also had an effect on the adult population. Memories of the horrendous conditions soldiers had to endure and the many casualties during the First World War meant there was little enthusiasm to volunteer. Later, men were conscripted, and their meagre allowance was two shillings a day (later increased to three shillings), part of which, for married men, had to be allocated to their wives. At least they were fed, clothed and accommodated, but many women were reduced to poverty. Some had to undertake poorly paid menial work to provide for their children. Later on in the war, women as well as men were conscripted to the war effort, some to the Forces, some to work in factories or on the land.

Many parts of the UK suffered intensive air-raids. The air-raid wardens, ambulance drivers and nurses did valiant work helping people who had been bombed out, some buried under collapsed buildings.

Civilians were expected to undertake fire-watching duties, unless their work or age made them exempt. For many, the air-raid sirens meant making their way to a shelter in their own house or garden, or elsewhere. The London Underground stations were considered some of the safest places, and after the early days when people fought for somewhere to settle, some even sleeping on the escalators, tiered bunks were installed on platforms. Those who qualified were allocated their own spot. This led to a breaking down of barriers and much fellowship, with communal singing and entertainment.

For the wives or girlfriends of men serving overseas there was the added anxiety of waiting for the postman with a letter from their beloved. Or a dreaded telegram might arrive to announce that a man was killed or missing, with the long wait for further information. Many men were taken prisoner by the Germans, Italians and Japanese: the last treated prisoners so viciously that many never returned and others were scarred for life.

When the war ended in 1945 there were jubilant celebrations on Tuesday, 8 May, VE (Victory in

Europe) Day, and on 14 August, VJ (Victory over Japan) Day, and gradually men (and women) were repatriated. Some, however, found it very difficult to adjust to civilian life. Other people had taken over their former jobs, and in spite of war service the returners might be considered inferior; their children had changed beyond recognition in their absence; and wives who had been working did not want to lose their independence. Because the starving millions in Europe had to be clothed and fed, rationing was at first more severe than in wartime and did not finally end until 1954.

The basic petrol ration was restored in June 1945 but continued to be rationed until 1950; clothes were rationed until 1949. Gradually life returned to normal: those children who had been evacuated returned home, but life would never be the same.

Ann Power was one of five children; although London was their home the family did not live there during the war:

When war was declared I was six years old; the family — Mum, Dad, two brothers, two sisters and I — were on holiday at Middleton-on-Sea. It was generally thought bombing would start immediately, so we extended the lease on our holiday home. When the owners wished to return after six months, we moved to a rented house, Tunmore Farm, in East Horsley, Surrey. Again the owners returned and we moved a mile or so down the road to St Kilda's. A third time the owners wanted the house for themselves, so my father bought a large thatched house with a beautiful garden, again in East Horsley.

Father's business manufactured margarine and bakery products, but he was also a Flight-Lieutenant in the Air Training Corps (ATC). Many of the boys he trained went into the RAF, and he was extremely upset during the Battle of Britain, when so many of them were killed.

To overcome the petrol shortage, my father had a gas-bag attached to the roof of his car, so he could drive down to Horsley from London most nights. Often he had friends with him who had been bombed out of their homes. At one time 19 people were living in our house, Ridings. They included lots of children and we were very free as our parents were so busy. Our own war effort included a waste-paper round with a wheelbarrow on Saturday mornings, collecting newspaper from all the houses on the way to the depot in the village. We also had an allotment of children's gardens, and I learnt to grow fruit and vegetables. In the autumn we collected hips from the hedges (2d a pound) and conkers (15s a hundredweight): these we took to a depot at school. Our payment was a long time coming, so my mother called on the headmistress and was told it had gone towards a school typewriter. Mother exploded — and we got out our hard-earned pocket money.

There were no sweets in the shops during the first year or two of the war; then we were issued with a sheet of sweet coupons, two ounces a week. Suddenly the corner-shop by Horsley Towers was full of unbelievable jars of sweets. I chose two ounces of raspberry drops the first week and thought they were magic. I and my elder sisters went into Guildford by train to school each day and had quite a walk at the other end. If the air-raid warning went, we had to choose a house and ask if we could sit in their shelter until the All Clear. In spite of rationing we were often given drinks and biscuits, so we rather enjoyed these occasions.

One year we went to a guest-house in Fittleworth, Sussex, for our holidays. The day after we arrived two army lorries full of German soldiers stopped in the village. Everyone was terrified until we realised they spoke English and were, in fact, dressed up for a military exercise.

Once, when the news was bad, I asked my father: "What will happen if we lose the war?" He replied that we wouldn't, so of course I had no worries on that score!

Joan Preston was one among thousands of London children who were evacuated to the country at the beginning of the war. They were to find themselves in entirely different surroundings — some pleasant, some not so pleasant:

Hazel and I were evacuees from working-class families in Tottenham, London, about ten years old and both only children. I can remember very clearly standing on the village green at Clavering, Essex, that afternoon in September 1939. The bus had carried us from a railway station to the village school, where we had been given

5

orange squash and shortbread biscuits. Then lists were brought out and marked by our teachers, and people, mostly ladies, came and took us away in twos or threes. Hazel and I were possibly the last two and we waited apprehensively.

Our teacher told us that we were very lucky and were going to stay with the family that lived opposite the green in The Old House. She introduced us to Mrs Luckock, who took our hands and led us to the oak-studded front door. There were rosemary bushes behind chains on either side. The door opened into a tiled hall with panelled doors at intervals and a large carved staircase, one great wall of which was covered with an oil painting depicting a battle scene.

She opened the first door on the right to reveal what seemed to me an endless room with bay windows and window seats. A large oval table took up the middle of the room and at this, having nursery tea, sat four children (including a baby in a high chair) and two ladies in starched blue and white uniforms — one older and plumper than the other. Mrs Luckock said, "Here are Hazel and Joan from London, who have come to live with us." Nanny smiled welcomingly and asked if we would like to wash our hands at the basin at the far end of the room.

As we passed the table we heard Thomas, the eldest boy, ask distinctly in an accent we could only call "posh", "May I have a rusk and butter and marmalade, please?" At the wash-basin Hazel and I looked at each other, quite dumbfounded. I believe it was I who whispered, "Two nurses!"

Tea in the upper-class nursery was completely new to us. Among the things we children could put on our bread (or rusks) were hundreds and thousands, but the first slice had to be just bread and butter. (Once, when I had earned Nanny's disapproval by boasting about a naughtiness I had committed at school, I was made to eat *all* my slices buttered only.)

I wasn't homesick, although I loved my parents and we corresponded warmly. Nanny was my guiding light and I respected and loved her. Hazel and I half-believed that the parting at the back of her hair was an extra eye! She understood us and teased us caringly.

The bedroom that Hazel and I shared had one high bed and one low one. I once tugged the bell pull, and we listened overawed at the bell ringing far away on a board down in the servants' quarters; later we saw the board with names of all the rooms printed below the bells.

It seemed a well-run household. We were scarcely ever allowed in the drawing-room, but our host and his wife would receive their two eldest children there and read to them each evening before they went to bed.

Our host was a gentleman farmer who had seen service in India; he was very handsome and was an important member of the Local Defence Volunteers (LDV). Hazel and I sometimes walked along hedged lanes to deliver messages to other members. One gave me my first peach, not from a tin, and I wondered at the carved beauty of the stone.

Mrs Luckock was a gracious, lovely-looking lady, especially when she called into the bedrooms of her four children, and us, to say goodnight before she was whisked off to a fancy dress ball as "Harriet-who-burnt-herself-with-matches". She lifted her trooped skirt to show the lacy pantaloons.

We were brought up with the children, Thomas, 8, Joanna, 7, Andrew, 3, and Elizabeth, the baby, but we did not go to the children's parties or share their riding lessons. We were older and helped the war effort by collecting salvage. We were given boiler suits to do this and some of the village boys helped us. We went to the village school but were taught by our own London teachers. We played Robin Hood games and teased the boys, who looked up to the London girls. Nanny teased us in turn when she found a love letter. Little Andrew imitated our cockney accents — asking for "kike" instead of "cake".

We had occasional visited from our parents — mine managed to run a car and liked the day out.

When we passed the scholarship we were moved to a nearby town and life was very different. Tottenham High School had been evacuated to a double-fronted, flint-faced house in the Quaker town of Saffron Walden. I believe only the first three years of the school were there. Thus it was a fairly personal education and I certainly felt that my teachers knew me and I them quite well. Miss E wore patterned coloured stockings, kept goats and accused me of being "a lily of the field who neither toiled nor spun" but was always well turned out. (My mother was a tailor and made most of my school uniform, which looked rather "designer" by comparison to that worn by the other children.)

When we first came to Saffron Walden, Hazel and I

were billeted on the landlord and lady of a back-street public house. However, after a few weeks someone decided that we should be moved, and we were.

Mrs Stoneman was an old lady who lived in a very pleasant detached house in a residential area of Saffron Walden. She must have been in her seventies and did not want two 11-year-old evacuees to live with her. Hazel and I were given jobs to do, and we hated the other lodger, an elderly gentleman, who was given much of our food ration. We were not unhappy: school was more important and we could giggle together at the behaviour of Mrs S and Mr H. Nevertheless, Hazel's doting mother eventually called her home to Tottenham, where the High School reopened. I stayed on alone for the rest of that year.

Christine Powell lived in many different homes:

I was three years old when the war began. It was a hard time for our parents, with rationing and utility points, the black-out and fear. Fear for your life, for your family, friends and neighbours, and the trauma of losing your home and possessions — as we did.

My father worked for the National Provincial Bank and had been moved from Wales to a branch in Liverpool. My parents rented a house in the suburbs. The rent was 30 shillings (£1.50) a week, quite a large sum at that time, but Dad was earning £5 weekly and could afford it.

Whenever the sirens went, I was yanked out of bed, put into my pink siren suit to keep warm, and together we would sit huddled under the stairs till the All Clear was sounded. We had to move from this house about two years later as a land-mine was dropped at the end of our road, shattering all the windows within a mile radius.

By the time we moved I was old enough to start school. My father had managed to get us a flat within the Liverpool area — I don't remember exactly where. How my parents were able to keep finding accommodation for us I will never know; there were so many homeless people. Much of London was destroyed in the war, but Liverpool fared almost as badly. Our next "home" was a guest-house at Hoylake. Father and I would walk on the sands of Dee on a summer Sunday evening. There were huge concrete blocks among the foreshore to stop the "bloody Jerries" landing.

I developed German measles and was confined to my room for some time. Then we moved again, I think because my father obtained a rented house in West Kirby. Mother wasn't at all happy with this place, but we were lucky to get anywhere. It was owned by a Catholic family and, as mother put it, there were "Hail Marys" on every mantelpiece. The walls were covered with pictures of Christ, and large and small crosses were everywhere. Mother was an atheist. Many times she cried out in anger, "If there's a God, why has he done this terrible thing to me?"

We must have stayed in these surroundings for a few years. I would come home from school on a winter's night, sit by a blazing fire, toasting fork in hand, and toast crumpets while listening to Children's Hour. While we were in West Kirby I almost died from scarlet fever. Probably Mother should have let me go to the fever hospital, but for some reason she did not, and I took three months to recover. Other local children were going down with it and returning to school. I just kept on getting relapses. The days when I was well enough, I would sit up in bed playing with paper cut-out dolls.

Once I was well, my room had to be fumigated, doors and windows sealed and something placed into the room that let off a vapour. Not long after this we were on the move again. My mother's nerves were in a bad way and she and I went to stay with her unmarried sister, Aunty Betty, in Oxford.

Father managed to get a transfer from the Liverpool bank to a branch in Southsea, so Mother was able to return to her roots. Here I was sent to a private school, Grindlwald. Sadly I didn't learn much there. Because I had missed so much schooling and attended so many different schools I still had difficulty in reading at the age of nine. We were taught French, arithmetic, reading, writing — the usual subjects. I must have been a very naughty child as I was always being sent to stand outside the classroom door.

Soon the end of the war was in sight, however. I stood on the sea-front cheering with the crowds on VE Day. I did not understand all that was going on: I just knew that everyone was happy.

When the war with Japan came to an end I was nearly ten years old. Father lost his job and Mother had a mental breakdown. Father was not able to look after me while Mother was in hospital, where they gave her "shock" treatment (ECT). My Aunt Molly and my grandmother invited me to live with them on the Isle of Wight. I loved being with them, and of course it meant no school again for several months. Living on the island was one of the happiest times of my life.

Mother came out of hospital six months later and I left my father's family and returned to Portsmouth. I did not continue going to the private school but went to the nearby elementary one for a short time. We had had to give up the flat we rented. My parents separated, Dad going to Nottingham, where he went to live with his aunt and uncle. He took a job in a hospital. Mother and I moved into a set of rooms at the back of the King's Theatre, where I developed a love of ballet, opera and musicals. On Saturdays and school holidays I would queue for the "gods" (gallery). I have some famous autographs: Dame Alicia Markova, Ivor Novello, Coral Browne, among others.

In 1949 we moved to Nottingham, as Mother was finding it difficult to manage alone. Thirteen is a difficult age at any time, and I found it hard to fit into life in a city involved in mining and industry after living near the sea. The grime, the buildings and the accents were quite a shock. Going to yet another new school was hard, too. Luckily for me, being an only child I had learnt to make friends easily and soon developed a friendship with a girl called Celia. We were both reasonably good at art, and dunces at most other subjects, so we were friendly rivals to be top in the class in art — and one of us was always bottom in maths, spelling, etc.

Growing up in the Forties was hard for some of us. But we did grow up, we had to. The Forties left my mother a very sad and bitter woman, but I can understand it, for she had had a lot to live through.

Gill Clay writes of life in Northern Rhodesia:

I was born in 1937. My father worked as a District Commissioner in the Colonial Service in Northern Rhodesia (now Zambia). For the first seven years of my life we lived on "outstations" — small administrative settlements hundreds of miles from shops, schools, civilisation. In the district of Isoka on the Tanzanian border our nearest European neighbours were missionaries on the mission station and hospital 60 miles away. When they were sick or injured the local people used to come to my mother, who did her best with her Girl Guide First Aid training. Her worst case was a girl who had had part of her bottom bitten away by a crocodile. My father was away and the rivers were in flood, so she had a nightmare drive to the hospital. A few months later the girl walked miles from her village to thank her.

I was four before I met another little girl of my own age who spoke English. At about the same age I saw crowds of men leaping round a dead man-eating lion which the game-guard had shot. I was convinced it would come alive again and pounce on us, so I took myself off to the lorry in great haste.

During the war years my brothers and I had very few manufactured toys, but we made our own amusements and had a wonderfully happy outdoor life. We had some children's books, and our first impressions of Britain were formed by the illustrations in the *Flower Fairies* and books by A. A. Milne, Beatrix Potter and Alison Uttley. My mother taught me, using a correspondence course and, having no shops, we used to dress up and play shops in order to learn about money, which never entered our lives at that time.

My father fixed the radio to the battery of the car every evening and we were told to hush as the pips were followed by "This is the BBC: here is the news." My grandparents wrote to say that if there were an invasion and they were killed, they had buried the silver and valuables in a certain place in their garden. Had Britain been overcome, the responsibilities of administrators in the Colonial Service would have been even more awesome. Fortunately, my mother's knitting parties with the local women to knit socks for soldiers were the only other reminder of the war. We loved to have visitors, which was a thrilling and rare occasion. Imagine, then, the excitement when convoys of Army lorries from South Africa came through on our rough gravel road, filled with hordes of dusty, sweaty, thirsty (English-speaking) soldiers on their way to the East African campaign in Abyssinia.

We had two holidays in Durban, South Africa, where I was astonished at the magic of civilisation: electricity and plumbing and lifts and stairs. I developed scarlet fever and chickenpox, followed by rheumatic fever, and had to be left behind in hospital for several months, desperately bored, lying on my back without toys, books or education. The only treatment for rheumatic fever in those days was complete rest. I rejoined my family in Lusaka, the capital, where my third brother was born, and we celebrated the end of the war.

A few months later we sailed on a troopship to England, where we enjoyed a wonderfully exciting winter of snowmen, snowballs and skating on the pond. I was devastated when my parents and little brothers returned to Zambia, leaving my eldest brother and me with our grandparents for three years to go to school in England. I was eight and a half and had only had two weeks at school before, but my best friend had a pony and I learnt to ride and became pony-mad like all my friends, reading books such as *Black Beauty* and *Moorland Mousie.* A delightful young girl looked after us and took us for walks and picnics, helped me to look after my rabbit, and taught us crafts and nature lore.

When I was 11 my parents came on leave and took us all back to the Zambian Copperbelt, where we were stationed. My wildest dreams came true when I was given a cocker spaniel puppy, and we had a family pony. I had a halcyon year at home before going off to boarding school, five days' train journey away in South Africa (schooling ended early in Zambia in those days). So my true childhood finished with the end of the Forties. I was lucky to grow up in those days without television and with few toys. We were the happier for having to develop our own resources.

Louise Boreham lived in a tenement in Edinburgh:

I was born in 1939 but my mother died just before war was declared, leaving my father with a three-month-old baby to care for. His own mother was in her sixties and not up to looking after such a small baby, so one of my maiden aunts came to stay as "housekeeper". Since the flat had only three rooms, I had to share a bed with her once I outgrew my cot. However, as I only ever knew Auntie and Daddy, I thought the other families were the oddities.

Since my Grannie lived in the same street, I used to go there if I came home and there wasn't anyone in our house, or I would try our next-door neighbour, or the one down the "stair" — I was never short of somewhere to go — and there were usually sweets or cakes there.

As my father was nearly 39 when war broke out and a single parent with a small baby, he was not called up into the Forces, but was engaged in essential war work. He had to take his turn at fire-watching, which meant being up all night making sure that the wood-working factory did not catch fire as a result of enemy action.

Three of my mother's brothers were in uniform. One had joined the RAF as a boy entrant and rose to be acting Wing Commander looking after the signals in the Gulf; another was in the Army and took part in the Normandy landings, but the third succeeded in getting himself invalided out because of his stomach ulcer. My two younger aunts were also dragooned into war-related work, pressing new uniforms and doing laundry work. Their mother, my other grandmother, never kept very well and I used to accompany Auntie most days to help her with housework. This involved a tram or bus ride, as she lived in a new council house on the outskirts of the town. The key was always on a string behind the door and we let ourselves in.

One of my other aunts met a Canadian sailor in the

Palais de Danse and eventually married him. He survived the dangers of the North Atlantic and took my aunt back to Canada, with their baby son.

I loved to play among the broken costume jewellery and spilt powder in my aunt's bedroom, but that was not popular with Auntie! My uncle, who was at home and a trained signwriter, scratched a living from doing up bicycles and selling them. It was better not to ask where they came from! My grandfather, who had died 12 years earlier, had been a sculptor and artist, and some of his oil paintings were still around. Unfortunately, my uncle covered the canvases with his own efforts, using the paint he put on the bikes. My indulgent grandmother made no attempt to stop him.

During the war, we often had to descend to the air-raid shelter in the back green when the siren sounded. After the hostilities ended, we played in a virtual warren of tunnels which had been built under a public park near us. We never thought of the danger of being totally lost in the dark labyrinth, or of a collapse of one of the tunnels.

As my Dad was a keen cyclist, I was bought a shiny new pale blue BSA bicycle, but it was too big for me at first and he had to fit blocks on the pedals. After many skinned knees and a burst lip, I mastered the art of balancing on two wheels and naturally wanted to play with it in the street like my pals, but this was not allowed. It was only for using on proper cycle runs with Dad. Not to be denied the pleasure of rushing through the air, I would ride anyone's bike I could get hold of, usually one too big for me.

One excursion we made frequently was to the allotment,

a couple of miles along the canal. People had been given the use of the empty site to encourage them to "Dig for Victory". We grew potatoes and other vegetables, soft fruit and some strawberries, but Dad always said he had heavy clay, the worst soil on the site, because his plot was next to the canal. So we used to gather sheep's "purls" on a nearby golf course and he steeped them in water to make a liquid manure. In winter we collected leaf mould to improve the consistency of the soil. However, the soil quality was not the only demoralising aspect of the allotment. The lads from the local reform school used to delight in pushing the old chest where Dad kept his tools into the canal. Then there would be a phone call to our neighbour (who had one of the two phones out of nine flats in the "stair") and Dad would have to go out and drag the heavy chest from the water and dry out all the implements. Who says vandalism is a new phenomenon?

CET was one of many small children who had to move when air-raids threatened:

When the war began we were living on the east coast of England. I was four. My parents decided it would be safer to move elsewhere to avoid the direct enemy attack they were anticipating. It was very difficult to find living accommodation, but my father discovered a 500-year-old house with shuttered windows and thick stone walls standing empty in Somerset. The house, which was in a terrible state of disrepair, belonged to the Lord of the Manor and was available to rent. It was believed that the thickness of the walls and the fact that it was situated at the foot of a high rock overlooked by woods made it comparatively safe from enemy attack. However, we had a few breakages, including my favourite doll, from a couple of bombs which fell, possibly accidentally, and left craters in a nearby field. Sometimes we collected kindling from the woods to light the coal fires, which were our only means of heating.

The house was damp, having stood empty for some time — and the lighting was sparse. We had gas-lights in the main living-rooms, with a shilling slot meter at the far end of the winding side-passage. As we had no electricity, ironing was either with the old flat-iron or with the gas-iron. The latter had two rows of gas jets down each side and constituted a fire risk, as the gas jets would flare if the iron was moved too quickly.

Unfortunately only a few rooms had gas lighting, so it was supplemented by small oil-lamps and candles. Each night I went up the wooden, winding staircase to bed, carrying a candle, which fell out of its holder at times, leaving me in pitch darkness. Occasionally, when it was bitterly cold, we used paraffin heaters: one of these caught fire in the back bedroom, covering everywhere with black soot and creating considerable consternation. The darkness, enhanced by the black-out, together with the flickering lights and shadows, and the creaking of the stairs, meant that I was often frightened. I never felt "at home" in my own home. There was no bathroom, but there was an upstairs toilet. The bath was an old tin tub in front of the kitchen fire.

At the back of the house, separated by a green baize

door, was the kitchen with its high wooden dresser; adjoining this was the scullery. As the floor of the scullery was flagstones, anything to be kept cold was simply kept on the stone floor. This meant that milk, collected daily in a jug from the local dairy, was kept at floor level. Any hot water had to be heated on the gas stove. Therefore, baths or washdays were a major upheaval. Leftover food was taken to a community bin known as the "pig bin". This exuded a terrible stench, but the food was supposedly to feed farm animals.

My father worked in the local Food Office, supplying people with ration books. At this time, crime had a different guise. Sometimes we were abruptly woken in the middle of the night by two local policemen, as the Food Office had been broken into and ration books stolen. (A black market was in existence.)

During the war I had taken rationing for granted and was quite concerned when it eventually ceased, thinking that there would not be sufficient food for everyone. In the mid-Forties small treats began to appear. A local news-agent was the first to sell ice-cream, and queues formed quickly for this new excitement. There were queues everywhere. On Saturday mornings I queued for cakes at the bakery, and then joined further queues at the butcher's and fishmonger's. Bananas began to appear and were devoured avidly by hungry youngsters, some of whom tried to eat the skin as well.

During wartime, toys were sparse. I had a small doll and also a pink desk, where I spent time writing, drawing and making ration books and clothing coupons for my dolls. By my mid-teens, all manner of toys appeared in the shops to my utter fascination: I had never dreamed of such luxuries.

There had been various fears for a small girl during the war, even for one who lived in the country. The darkness on the roads was frightening, as sometimes I had to run through the country lanes, where the trees and bushes cast long eerie shadows in the moonlight, to fetch a doctor for my sick mother. However, when the street lamps were lit at the end of the war, it concerned me deeply. With my child's understanding I did not fully comprehend the meaning of victory. I felt sure that the street lights and the removal of black-outs would enable the enemy to resurge and attack us. However, I gradually realised that "victory" meant a complete cessation of enemy attack and my trepidation ended.

Although Bristol was George Moore's home, the family spent part of the war in Cardiff, returning to Bristol in 1942:

I was nine when the Forties began. My father, who worked as a representative for Franklyn Davy, a branch of the Imperial Tobacco Co., was posted from Bristol to Cardiff, and in February we all moved into a new house on the outskirts of the city. When the phoney war ended my father responded to Eden's call and joined the Local Defence Volunteers, later called the Home Guard. He and his unit spent much time guarding an entrance to Cardiff via a narrow country lane near our home. Their only weapon to begin with was one ancient Ross rifle without a bolt action.

One night, at the time of Dunkirk, he was called out with others to help unload two hospital trains that had arrived at a Cardiff suburb station. Some of the men were walking wounded and were out on the streets of Cardiff each day in their hospital blues. Two were brought home most afternoons for tea and a seat in a comfortable chair. Their stories, no doubt embellished, entranced me.

The Battle of Britain followed. Although Cardiff was far from the main area of activity, raids and alerts were regular, so much school time was spent in the shelters.

In the middle of all this activity I had a personal crisis. In September 1940 I went down with appendicitis, coupled with peritonitis. With a full raid alert on, I had to be moved one night from home to Llandoch Hospital, between Cardiff and Penarth, for an immediate operation. I was in hospital for a month and away from school until the end of the year.

When the heavy blitz began that winter my sister and I were placed under a bed lifted on to chairs. This was placed against a secure inner wall of the house. Under this was a mattress and there we remained until the All Clear. My father would be watching outside, dealing with incendiaries, whilst my mother watched the house in case one landed on our roof. If we heard the whistle of a heavy explosive bomb coming too close for comfort, she threw herself under the bed with us. When the siren sounded the dog and cat were often *in situ* in the shelter before we children. They had rapidly learnt what all the noise was about.

When our school was destroyed in a raid we spent part of the time at home hunting for shrapnel and unexploded incendiary bombs. When intact these weighed about two pounds. Much energy was spent throwing them at a brick wall to see if they would "go off". Adult outrage coupled with a clip around the ear soon brought this activity to a halt!

In June 1941 my father was called up and set off on a late-night train for Blackpool to join the RAF. He trained as an engine fitter. The following year my mother returned to Bristol so that she could go to work in my father's firm. We moved into a flat in Henleaze.

Life was enlivened in 1942 with the arrival of the American forces. Many thousands were based in and around Bristol. They were billeted, for sleeping purposes only, in private homes around our neighbourhood. There was no choice. People had to clear "surplus rooms" and take them in. The American forces provided all the furniture. Nobody really minded: the necessity was understood. Indeed, many friendships were made from those days that still exist today.

To the children the Americans were a source of sweets (candy and gum). There were also many other examples of their typical generosity. The Americans' strange games of baseball and their version of football were observed with delight. Later, when we reached the period before and after D-Day there was added interest, with huge military convoys passing through our streets by night and day, going to the nearby Avonmouth Docks. Also there was a huge tank park covering half of the nearby Durdham Downs. All of this was watched avidly, and sometimes we were given rides in Sherman tanks.

My father was posted overseas to West Africa in 1942. In 1943, at the height of the war, British servicemen could be posted there for not more than 18 months — it was called "the white man's grave". Whilst my father was there he had five bouts of malaria and was very ill when he came home. He was given immediate sick leave for a month. The air base on which he served is now the main tourist airport for the Gambia.

Before returning to school in January, during the bitter winter of 1947, I recall being despatched to Eastville gas-works with a sack and a trolley. I was accompanied by friends, each of us told to collect coke. There, shivering, we stood in a long queue to take a turn under the shute. It was necessary to catch the still-warm fuel in the sack, during which operation we were smothered in dust. Then it was a three-mile walk and push home. The grim early months of 1947 were followed, however, by an excellent summer, and many of the previous hardships were forgotten.

Vivienne Hubbard was brought up in the Birmingham area:

My parents both came from united families in neighbouring mining villages. For both, the chapel had been the centre of their social and religious life. They were demonstratively affectionate to each other, and to us, which provided a security not shared by all my peers. Once, when Dad kissed Mum in the presence of a visitor, my small brother said in tones of some disgust, "They are always at it."

24

I was the elder child. My brother arrived five years later. In spite of, or perhaps because of, the gap in our ages we were always very fond of each other and did things together. When we were small my mother was indefatigable in reading us stories, which we loved. Dad composed his own stories and romped with us. We listened to the radio as a family to serial stories like *Barlash of the Guard*, about the Napoleonic Wars, and to wartime programmes like *ITMA* and, of course, to the ncws. The radio news was supplemented by TV pictures at the end of the Forties, when Dad bought a television set.

Dad took politics very seriously and had us all busy addressing Labour Party envelopes before delivering them. When young, we collected numbers at polling stations and later went canvassing.

On Sunday evenings we went to chapel together. Meals were always a family occasion except for the necessary disruption when Dad was on nights making munitions. He was strict, but very caring. When we were ill and needed medicine he always tasted it himself first before administering the dose, followed by a sweet. He taught us generosity by example, always sharing everything out among the family and by befriending neighbours and old folks in trouble.

I lived with my grandparents in the village of Wales for a while during the blitz, in their 16th-century cottage. It rejoiced in one cold-water tap and a well in the garden. There was gas lighting downstairs in some rooms. For the rest, wax candles were our only illumination. Bathing was in a tin tub specially filled for the occasion, but I was sent to an aunt who had a modern bathroom. Cooking was done in an oven heated by a coal fire, in which my grandmother produced toothsome homemade bread and cakes.

Holidays were spent with relatives during the war. When possible, for Christmas we went by tram, steam train and bus to the larger family in Sheffield, where a succession of grandparents and aunts fed us with the best they could muster, including the delicacy of chicken, as both sets of grandparents kept fowls. After 1945 we went on summer family holidays to various seaside places, which we explored on foot and by bus. Boarding houses could not be lavish and my parents had to go scouring in cafés at night to fill up their hungry youngsters.

Mother worked very hard. Before her marriage she was a headmistress, but on marriage in 1932 she was forced to stop teaching, as it was a career banned to married ladies. As soon as my brother was four, however, she returned to teaching: women were needed in schools in the absence of the men at war. Henceforth she looked after the home *and* taught.

Ian Sandeman saw aspects of the war from the Isle of Wight:

I was 11 at the outbreak of war. I'd been born in Exeter and had lived from the age of one in Ryde on the Isle of Wight, this being my home until 1950. The family home was a Georgian house and garden, the property of my grandmother. For its day the house had many "mod cons", including a wireless set and an Electrolux vacuum cleaner that lasted until the Seventies. We also had a clothes' iron heated by gas, but no refrigerator. The house was heated by gas and coal fires. We had bicycles but no car. The household comprised my grandmother, my mother and an elderly "Nannie". My father had left the scene about the time I was born, and Mother made considerable sacrifices to give my only brother and me a good start in life. I had no sisters.

In Ryde we well knew that we would never be a target for the enemy. In fact, from our first-floor windows we used to watch Portsmouth burning during its ordeal — until one night early in 1943 when a disabled German aircraft jettisoned its bombs on Ryde. Thereafter we took refuge in our Anderson "table" shelter in our basement. Food rationing was a continual talking-point. Mother did the housekeeping and we never went short, although her ingenuity was tested during that period.

Mother arranged for me to spend some of my summer holiday of 1942 at a boys' camp in Northamptonshire, where we spent each day helping with the harvest. There I first encountered Italian prisoners of war, also working on the land, some of whom were living "on parole" with the farmers and their families. The few I spoke to were thoroughly glad to be out of the fighting and enjoying a relatively comfortable existence.

Early in the war the Isle of Wight became a restricted area, at first because of the danger of invasion by the Germans, and later due to the increasing military activity during the build-up to the Allied invasion of Europe. Civilian access was restricted to those whose homes were on the Island, and our identity cards were checked on

27

entering and leaving. Access to the beaches was at school forbidden to us as they were cordoned off with various obstacles intended to impede invaders.

By 1944 the harbours and creeks of the Island became jammed with landing craft of every type, and that spring saw the assembly of a vast armada which filled the whole Solent area. We were puzzled by the sight of huge "blocks of flats" being built on the opposite shore of the Solent. Only after D-Day did we realise that they were destined to become part of the Mulberry Harbours established on the Normandy coast. I was at school in Somerset on the night of 5 June, when I saw and heard another armada — Allied aircraft — flying low overhead on their way to Normandy. Neither before nor since have I witnessed such an incessant stream of aircraft.

Audrey Dench remembers her sister's wartime wedding:

One of my sisters decided for some unknown reason (she had been engaged for years) to get married in 1943 just when things were getting really scarce. I don't know where she got her dress from, maybe she had some coupons to spare. A friend and I were bridesmaids in borrowed blue dresses and luckily it was a gorgeous hot April day. The reception was held at a restaurant at the Arding & Hobbs store at Clapham Junction. The food was the best that the caterers could manage, a cold collation of tasteless ham with a bit of salad, and the wedding cake was made of sponge and covered in an ersatz (to coin a German phrase in fashion at the time) chocolate icing.

However, it was a splendid day and the happy couple departed on honeymoon.

Nina Armour describes being bombed out:

Some time in autumn 1941 I was at school, aged 14, in the peaceful Hertfordshire countryside when I received a letter from my mother, telling me that our home was no more. An incendiary bomb had fallen on our flat — the top floor of a Victorian house in a street of many similar houses in St John's Wood, London. Our road, Alexandra Road, ran parallel to the main Euston railway-line which was, no doubt, a target.

The incendiary bomb had split into three, I was told later, one part landing on my bed. The flat was wrecked, if not by fire, then by water. The roof had collapsed on to the remains of our belongings, including Mother's treasured Blüthner grand piano. The fire-fighters must have left it very wet, and after that it rained for three weeks, almost non-stop, on the roofless flat before Blüthners could get to the piano and remove it for storage and eventual repair after the war.

After we had lost our home Aunt Loulie, who lived near Lords Cricket Ground not far away, arranged for my mother and Aunt Nina to move into her neighbour's house as caretakers. The owners had moved to their country house for the duration of the war, so my mother and aunt moved into the servants' part of the house. In one of the main rooms stood a grand piano, on which we were welcome to play, and I enjoyed that when I stayed there during the school holidays.

In the garage were stored the few rescued items from our former home: some charred and all smelling of smoke. Some of these were cleaned and polished and used again when Mother and I had another flat, in Abbey Road. This was when I left school in 1943.

When the war ended, my mother went to Berlin with the Control Commission as an interpreter at the many conferences which took place there. I was studying textile design at the Central School of Art and Craft, and it was decided to let the flat to an RAF officer and his wife. I went into digs near some cousins in Hampstead Garden Suburb in north London. However, after about a year I came back to the flat and let two rooms to friends. During this time Blüthners returned the rebuilt piano, looking quite beautiful again and sounding wonderful, too.

During the severe winter of 1946-7, when there was a fuel shortage, gas pressure was sometimes so low that it was impossible to cook on the gas cooker. We still had some coal which we used in the Courtier all-night stove in the sitting-room. It had doors that opened, and we fried sausages over the hot coals.

Frost caused problems, too, and pipes froze. I repaired a leaking pipe by winding sticky tape round and round tightly. It lasted for years.

Muriel Lees has mixed memories of the war years in Moffat, Scotland:

I was the middle one of five children — Jean and Stanley were older, Andrew and Doris younger. We lived in a large council house, with a bathroom and a large garden. The kitchen had two sinks and a boiler — you lit a fire underneath to heat the water for the washing. There was also a walk-in larder and a coal-house.

I learnt to play the piano. The minister from the church often came to tea, as my father was a church elder, and I had to play for him. No games were allowed on Sundays, not even cards. We all went for a walk and Father wore a bowler hat. Mother was not allowed to wear lipstick and, of course, no woman entered a pub.

We attended Sunday School, church, choir and a Bible class at the Manse on a Sunday evening. The minister's wife used to make supper. Any entertainment was organised through the church, e.g. badminton in the church hall. The Sunday School party at Christmas was the highlight of the year.

My school years were very happy. Everyone could read and write, and we all respected the teachers — and also the police. It was a great disgrace for the police to come to your door. I remember once my brothers had taken a duck hut for a den down by the river. The policeman came to the door, marched them down to the river and made them pick it up and put it right back where they had taken it from. They also had to go and apologise to the owner. It was a lesson well learnt: they certainly did not do anything like that again.

In spite of food rationing, I was never hungry. We had porridge, broths, rabbit and "mince and tatties". I've never had a bad stomach in my life! I hated saccharine in my tea and have never taken sugar since. The only item a child could buy with a penny was a large cooking apple, and I've eaten my share of them.

At the end of the war everybody listened to the radio and danced in the High Street. Americans in a jeep threw coloured smoke-bombs about. There was much rejoicing.

In the terrible winter of 1946-7 cottages were completely buried in snow and we could jump over the telephone wires. I left school in 1949 and went to Glasgow and West of Scotland Commercial College. My first job was for British Road Transport in Glasgow as a shorthand typist. The wage was £2 5*s* per week. As my room and board came to £2 a week it left hardly anything to live on. On my 18th birthday I had my medical and joined the WRNS.

In 1947 Isla Forbes spent Christmas with her fiancé's family in Chelmsford. She was made very welcome but was daunted by the variety of skills she must now acquire:

The whole Brownless family, parents and five grown-up children, were at Moulsham Vicarage, thankful to be home again. Four of them had served abroad for most of the war. With new jobs in civvy street and David just off to join the South Africa Police, the unspoken thought was whether this might be their last Christmas together. It was a busy time for Grandma Brownless, planning and cooking for at least eight of us and various visitors. Food was still rationed and one had to shop frequently to pick up any extras. There were queues and often the results of a shopping expedition were meagre.

The meals, cooked by Grandma, with help from Margaret, whose skill amazed me, were carried and trolleyed by all of us into the dining-room, a long way from the kitchen. After all this preparation and the hectic assembly of the family for grace ("Anyone seen David?" "Basil — where are you?" "Oh sorry, I was reading"), mealtimes were merrily formal round the large mahogany table, properly laid beforehand so there was no scrambling about once we were seated. Delicious food: Grandma was a genius foodwise and could knock up a pie in the time it would have taken me to weigh the flour. Grandpa Brownless, addressed as Pa, sharpened his knife as though preparing to execute a bishop, and carved at speed. Plates were passed to Grandma who served the vegetables, mostly grown in their own garden.

Pa gobbled, or so Grandma said, and she tried hard to slow him down. David ate steadily and never said a word. Basil always introduced a topic of great interest, which Roland or Philip picked up, and then Basil, all smiling innocence, would say something provocative about a modern hymn tune, or the Socialists, or perhaps Free-masonry. Grandpa readily fell into the trap, dismissing it as new-fangled nonsense, while Basil smilingly laid another snare for those who thought the opposite. Basil had his hands in his lap all this time, the better to concentrate on the conversation, Grandma would watch his unregarded food cooling and Margaret might say, "Get on with it, Basil", but not till everyone else had finished would he noticed anything but the talk. Then he would eat up, more quickly even than Grandpa. All this was fun, most stimulating, though I wonder if Grandma enjoyed it as much as we did. She was concerned about Grandpa, who had recovered from a serious cancer operation but whose heart required him to lead a quieter life than either the parish or his inclination allowed.

Afternoon tea was a great tradition, always with a beautiful tablecloth. There were home-made scones and cakes on the "curate's delight", an elegant, mahogany, three-tiered stand. How Grandma managed all these goodies on the rations, heaven knows!

After supper on Christmas Day we played silly games in the drawing-room. The one I remember best was suggested by Roland: we had in turn to name a patent medicine beginning with the letter A, progressing through the alphabet. Just aspirin would not do — it had to be a brand name like Aspro. Grandpa had a long memory of Victorian remedies, but Roland won easily.

Grace Horseman's experience of motherhood in 1946 was not easy:

During the war years there was little opportunity for me to enjoy family life. When I was at home, most of my time and energy went on work and on travelling there and back; when I was away I was either in digs or sharing a flat with colleagues. Then everything changed on 21 April 1945. I had a phone call from Ken Horseman, whom I had last seen in December 1940, shortly before his regiment of the Rifle Brigade was sent to Egypt. I had no idea he was back in England. He had been taken prisoner just before

Christmas 1941, and had been in POW camps in Italy and then Germany.

As an ex-POW Ken was given a week's leave, then another, and another until 16 June 1945, when the army suddenly granted him two weeks. We had been unofficially engaged, but out of the blue Ken's mother said, "Why don't you two get married? You can share our house until you can get your own." We were delighted at the thought of being together, so arranged a hasty Registry Office wedding, with just our parents as witnesses. With few coupons available I had to content myself with a new hat and blouse to wear and an old suit. Ken was granted no further leave, so our honeymoon consisted of one brief night in the country.

I continued working until Ken was to be discharged from the army on 28 February 1946 and left my job the same day. I was already nearly seven months pregnant and Ken was suffering from the effects of years of semi-starvation. Red Cross parcels had not got through during the Allied advance, and the Germans themselves were starving. For one whole week the prisoners survived on beetroots they had managed to scrounge. Ken never wanted to see a beetroot after that!

Then on Easter Sunday, 21 April 1946, our son Brian arrived two weeks prematurely. All went well until shortly before I was due to be discharged from St Thomas's Hospital. The wards were over-full and the nurses overworked. I contracted puerperal fever — quite painful and very unpleasant as it made me extremely depressed. I remember weeping copiously and saying to the Sister, "I don't know why I'm crying but I can't help it." She replied, "Don't worry. It is just part of the illness," but she did not tell me what it was and I did not discover until the health visitor came to see me at home.

Because of the overcrowding I was sent home prematurely with a baby whose bottom was purple with gentian violet. Brian suffered from acidosis, although it was two years before it was diagnosed. He never slept more than two hours at a time, day or night, and would wake up screaming with pain. With me recovering from puerperal fever and Ken with a gippy tummy, life was not easy.

In those days there was no special food for babies, so it all had to be sieved before it was given to them. Another problem was the shortage of soap and soap flakes (on ration and detergents not yet invented), which made the washing of nappies and other clothes difficult.

In late autumn 1947 we were entertaining friends to tea when there was a knock at the door. It was a doctor friend of my parents. Mother was recovering from pneumonia and I assumed the bad news was about her, but was told it was my father who had had an accident. I went to their home and was met on the doorstep by a policeman who, without any warning, escorted me down our cellar steps to see the body of my father lying on the floor at the bottom. I had not been told he was dead. Apparently he had fallen backwards whilst carrying a scuttle of coal up the cellar steps.

I stayed with Mother that night but then had to return to Brian and Ken. It was a very difficult time, particularly as my father had just agreed the sale of the house and it was too late to stop it.

Mother eventually decided to share a house with my

brother and his wife. It was 1950 before Ken and I were able to buy our own home, and soon after that Brian went to nursery school.

After being demobilised from the Army Keith Spooner found himself living in Manchester, a far cry from the Italy he had just left:

The Manchester where I found myself during the late Forties was a dour and dingy place, with "bombcrofts" still waiting to be cleared and built upon, even in the city centre. The general atmosphere was often of a grey-brown brume, damp soot evident on buildings, on pavements, even on the ubiquitous pigeons. The main thoroughfares, along which trams majestically swayed, had their gutters lined with barrowboys' mobile stalls, mostly exhibiting sooty produce. The flashier uses of plastic, veneers and neon had not yet transformed shop façades, which were solid and dignified, or drearily dun.

The city had a reputation for rain, but probably the average yearly rainfall was no greater than in many other areas of Britain. A week of Manchester's particular brand of sooty drizzle, however, would convince any visitor that the place was perpetually soaked. In warmer weather the air was humid, sun shafting laboriously through the industrial haze, an atmosphere more favourable to cotton than citizens — and King Cotton had built those imposing warehouses with their almost palatial appearance. Winter fogs were so thick and frowsty that it seemed you could cut chunks out of the surrounding murk. This phenomenon was to be classified as "smog" and was finally tackled by smoke abatement acts and so forth.

There were still to be seen human legacies from the darker days of the Industrial Revolution: near-dwarfs, people suffering from rickets, dropsy and goitres, mis-shapen inheritors of the cramped back-to-back housing with its outside privies, rushed up for the migration of agricultural workers to the mills and factories, and still widely inhabited.

The great mills that surrounded the area were lit up, and seemed after dark to be sailing under their smoke like liners. Cooling tower exhalations and chemical effusions mixed with the lowering elements to create dramatic sunsets. There was a sombre, smouldering beauty at such times; a certain grimy grandeur about this industrial landscape even by day, something less purely functional, more indigenous-seeming, than today's ferro-concrete, stressed steel and glass.

CHAPTER
TWO

School

Even before 3 September 1939 children were evacuated from London and other cities to areas that were considered to be less vulnerable to air-raids. They were billeted willy-nilly on welcoming or unwelcoming households, but accommodating them in schools was another matter. Often there was no room for additional pupils in the local school, so it meant "doubling up" — the original pupils attending in the morning and newcomers in the afternoon, or vice versa. Meanwhile, many school buildings in cities had been requisitioned for use by the Forces or other services, and when pupils began to drift back to their homes during the phoney war, there was no school for them to go to. Once the blitz started, many schools were bombed and often severely damaged, if not destroyed. Again accommodation had to be shared. Meanwhile, about 20,000 male teachers had been called up; many women who had been forced to give up their profession on marriage returned to help fill the vacancies, and newly-weds stayed on. For the first time boys in boarding and grammar schools were taught by women — and appreciated the experience. Elsewhere teachers were confronted with classes of 50 or more, whilst others had to work in church halls, or even hotels, with little equipment — sometimes no blackboard, books, paper or desks.

The shortage of paper was to affect everyone. Margins in exercise books were very narrow, or non-existent; some schools tried to overcome the difficulty by making the pupils first fill the book by writing in pencil, then turning it sideways and writing over the pencil in ink.

When sleep was interrupted overnight by air-raids, as frequently happened, particularly in the London area, many children missed part of school the following morning, without reprimand. If there were daylight raids, school took place in shelters; playing games replaced lessons. This was fun for the younger children, but not surprisingly the standard of education fell considerably during the war years.

As the war progressed, more and more schools reopened in London and other cities. Preparing for public examinations was a problem, and students often had permission to continue their studies in the classroom during an "alert", if they so wished. If there was a raid during the examination itself, students could continue the paper in a shelter, or wait in silence until the All Clear. The examination boards made allowance for the difficult circumstances by making sure that the percentage of passes corresponded to those of previous years.

School playing-fields were considered likely landing places for planes in the event of an invasion, so were put out of action by obstructions such as sewer pipes or pits. Those who disliked organised games were much more likely to escape them during the war.

The demand for labour during the war had one advantage: women with young children could be employed only if arrangements were made for the welfare of their offspring, so many wartime nursery places were provided. By 1943 65,000 children were attending nurseries. Mostly these were extremely well run, headed by trained personnel, and conditions were excellent. Each child had his or her own peg and pinafore; they played games, sang and had some lessons. They learned simple hygiene and how to dress, tie shoelaces and go to the lavatory unaided. A very healthy lunch was provided, after which they could have a rest if they wished. Factory and office hours were often long, so mothers could bring their children before breakfast and collect them after supper.

Once war ended, things gradually returned to normal but, as with housing, there was much rebuilding and redecorating to do. Only slowly did books and paper become available. Men returning from the traumas of war found it difficult to settle down to a life of teaching once more; some suffering from shell shock found it impossible.

* * *

In the Forties parents were not afraid to let their small children walk to school on their own, as Louise Boreham describes. Traffic was not heavy and little was heard of child molesters:

I went to the primary school in the next street to ours. From the age of five we walked to school with our friends, and no one bothered us. We certainly didn't want to be branded as "cissies" by having our mums (or Auntie in my case) accompanying us. My father had attended the same school at the beginning of the century and it did not appear to have changed much since then. Each of the three floors had a large space or hall with classrooms along one side. At each end were the stairs, one for the boys and one for the girls. Once we progressed from the infants on the ground floor to the upper levels, we had to march up these stairs while two female teachers hammered out the music on upright pianos at the top of each staircase. When I hear "Colonel Bogie", I don't think of *The Bridge over the River Kwai* but of our upward processions into the school.

Towards the end of our time there, the girls got sewing and knitting, while the boys went off to handicraft. How I wished I could have gone with them instead of being forced to sit and knit a Dutch bonnet in moss stitch, with number 12 needles and 4-ply wool. I used to stretch the work like mad in the hope that I'd be set free from the torture. The hand sewing was just as bad. If it wasn't perfect, the stitches had to be taken out and done again. One of my teachers used to tell me off for biting the thread instead of cutting it. She said I'd damage the enamel of my teeth, and bits would chip off. How I wish I'd listened to her!

Vivienne Hubbard's education was religious as well as secular:

I was seven at the start of the Forties. My education was somewhat hit and miss in 1940, but very varied. I lived in Birmingham with my parents and walked daily through the Bournville parks, passing the barrage balloon en route for school. Classes were interrupted by air-raid warnings and retreats to shelters, and by practices wearing our gas-masks. I recall inflicting painful blows unintentionally on passers-by as I swung along with the mask in its tin box. Later in the year I was sent for safety to live with my paternal grandparents in a village called Wales.

Here my education continued in the local school, where promotion was by ability and slower pupils were kept behind. I was quickly promoted and found myself in a class taught by an elderly lady, who had formerly taught my father. She had not been to college, but had learnt her craft as a pupil-teacher. Methods were not modern: we learnt to spell by chanting in unison, for example.

My religious education was not neglected. Each night Grandpa produced the Bible and I had to read aloud. Then we all knelt whilst the adults prayed. I realised that my grandfather was talking to a friend, and from then on I longed to know God as Grandpa did, though this was not to happen until I was in my twenties.

Two years later, when the blitz was over, I returned to

Birmingham and resumed a more normal education. I passed the examination to go to the grammar school, where I still was at the end of the Forties.

CET's first school was in Somerset, where she was evacuated with her parents:

When I started at the local primary school I had to wear a small disc around my wrist with my name, address and identity number, in case I got lost. (More sinisterly, such discs might have been needed to identify bodies injured or killed during an air-raid.) My gas-mask went with me in case there was an air-raid. Sometimes these gas-masks had to be worn inside the classroom. I once listened to a dramatic rendition of *Jack and the Beanstalk*, whilst feeling suffocated by my gas-mask. I cried at the horror of it, but the boys in the class tried to cheer me up by assuring me that the Giant was only a "pretend monster".

On happier occasions we were permitted a turn on the rocking-horse, but this never seemed to last long enough, which was scarcely surprising as there were 50 of us in the class. The teacher was said to be a strict disciplinarian of the old school, and the teaching was of necessity very formal, but the achievements were good and we all learned the basics.

From Infant School I progressed to the adjacent Church of England Junior School, where I stayed until I was 11. The school buildings were Dickensian, built to a rectangular plan with three classrooms on each side. The headmistress's house was in the middle and from this she had the dubious privilege of a view over the boys' playground. The classroom ceilings were high, and the tall arched windows were topped by such mottoes as: "Children, obey your parents!"

Nevertheless, the school was a happy one. The headmistress, a vivacious single lady, kept golden cocker spaniels which followed her everywhere. Whenever there were litters she would take the puppies round the classrooms for the children to admire. They were very gentle dogs and used to scramble under the desks to rub against our knees with their wet noses. Also, the school had a tabby cat who loved to perch on a teacher's high desk, gazing benignly at the children doing their sums, possibly anticipating playtime and some left-over milk from our milk bottles. At that time the Government supplied each child with a one-third of a pint of milk daily.

On VE Day I was taken to watch the procession in Bristol, standing very near the Lord Mayor's house. I also joined in some dancing at the bandstand on the sea front. My hair, then worn in plaits, was bedecked in red, white and blue ribbons.

The headmistress instituted a special "Pets' Day", when children were encouraged to bring their pets to school. These were many and varied, and were exhibited in the girls' playground. There were cats, rabbits, hamsters, tortoises and even a stick insect, which sadly died within its own matchbox — perhaps of fright or claustrophobia. Dogs were not officially allowed, but strangely some found their way to their owners and even managed to remain!

We were taken on nature walks, mainly through the woods, with some boys playing cowboys and Indians on

45

our return. We also walked around the cliffs and along coastal paths. Our treasures, whether of flowers or plants, pebbles or shells, were proudly displayed on the Nature Table. We were encouraged to write and illustrate a daily Nature Diary — and for this I won first prize.

At the end of the war, my parents decided to stay in Somerset and not return to the east coast. I joined an independent girls' school in Bristol, where I was one of a very few scholarship girls. The regime was considerably more restrictive than in the junior school and, although I did not enjoy it, the academic training was good.

Towards the end of the Forties, the school initiated exchange visits with a school in Münster, Germany. A German girl with marvellous English came to stay with me, which meant that I in turn joined a school trip to Münster in 1948. The long German working day amazed me, and I was staggered to witness the feverish rebuilding of cities such as Münster and Cologne. In Bristol the rate of rebuilding was considerably slower.

Peggy Brackenbury entered Clapham County Secondary School in 1938, but her years there were much affected by the war:

When my family hastily returned from holiday at the outbreak of war, Clapham girls had already been evacuated, so I joined my two younger brothers and spent September 1939 to July 1940 at Wallingford Grammar School. We were evacuated to Cholsey, Berkshire (now Oxfordshire). It was a bitterly cold winter and I had chilblains on my hands for the first and only time in my life.

Even as a 12-year-old I felt that the education at the Berkshire school was not as advanced as that of Clapham High School and Clapham County Secondary School, which I had attended before the war.

My host and hostess were kind, but did not seem to realise that a young girl approaching adolescence needed rather more food than they provided. I entered my teens feeling cold and a little hungry. Because of the lack of food my parents decided to bring me home to Balham during the phoney war. Of course, almost as soon as I returned to London the war began in earnest. How naive we were! One evening my mother called me into the garden to see the exceptionally beautiful "sunset". It was the reflection of the East End docks on fire.

I attended the South-West London Emergency School for Girls at Broomwood Road, Clapham, for two weeks. I learnt to write three ways on a piece of paper, as stationery was severely rationed. It took me years to use paper normally.

After the dog-fights in the sky over Croydon airport and incendiary bombs in a neighbouring garden, my father hurriedly arranged for our local grocer to drive me to Windsor to join my London school: Clapham County Secondary School had been evacuated to Windsor County Boys' School.

I loved the castle at Windsor, the river and being billeted near my best friend, Joan Walden. We walked up the Long Walk to the Copper Horse, or went to W. H. Smith's on the mornings when we had few lessons. One morning as we cycled to school, Joan and I saw a plane flying very low over our heads. The engine was on fire, but we cycled on, asking each other history questions, as we had a test with Mrs Rau later. Afterwards we were glad to read in the local paper that the pilot had bailed out safely in Windsor Great Park.

One wet Bank Holiday my host and hostess took their small son, my friend Beryl and myself for a walk in Windsor Great Park. Beryl and I were playing hide and seek in the bracken until the rain became so heavy that we decided to return home up the Long Walk. No one else had ventured out in such dismal weather. A sports car appeared with the King driving, and the Queen waved to us. We didn't care how wet we were after that!

We saw the two elder children of the Duke of Kent being conducted into church by their nanny. Later, one bleak morning we went to see the wreaths laid out by St George's Chapel, after the Duke of Kent was killed in a plane crash.

We were always very pleased when our hostesses gave us money to go to the British Restaurant in Eton for lunch. That meant we could mingle with the Eton boys walking to and from sculling practice on the river. We weren't supposed to talk to them, but one girl in our form got to know a few of them as she was billeted with an Eton master.

On the last day of the summer term, 1943, the County Boys' School hung banners from the school roof with the words "WE DON'T WANT TO LOSE YOU, BUT WE THINK YOU OUGHT TO GO" painted on them. They had been very hospitable.

Returning to Clapham was strange. Our staff had to take it in turns to patrol the building at night in case of incendiary bombs. In the summer of 1944 the V1 and V2 bombs started. I preferred the latter because you did not have to count before you heard them explode.

Isla Brownless (*née* Forbes) went to school at Wycombe Abbey till it was taken over by the Americans as their HQ in March 1942:

When we arrived in September 1939 we found 400 girls from St Paul's School, London, had joined the 360 girls already at Wycombe Abbey. Some of the Paulinas were allocated to WA houses and many were billeted in the town. The squash in classrooms and passages was unbelievable. As the Paulinas did not know their way around and nor did we as new girls, it took ages for a class to assemble in the right room. Whenever the bell rang, everyone debouched into the passages, not knowing where to go. Immense timetabling difficulties were only one aspect of the sudden amalgamation of the two schools. Of course there was rivalry: the Paulinas were cleverer than we were. At lacrosse, we ran rings roung them as they had never seen such huge playing fields. At netball they were supreme and we felt like elephants in a *corps de ballet* of eels.

As the phoney war produced few immediate bombs and as more youngsters were sent overseas, the Paulinas trickled away and the ghastly crush lasted only a few terms. Those who stayed became fully WA, their parents

49

hoping it was a safe area. When air-raids began in 1940, Lord Carrington's unused (fortunately) sewer across the field at Daws Hill was prepared as an air-raid shelter for the school. We began using it in pleasant September weather. When the siren went, we trooped up the hill to one of a dozen entrances. The staff policed our orderly descent down 70 boarded steps cut in the chalk. The tunnel was 40 feet down, 4 feet wide, 6 feet high, and several hundred yards long. The outside staff had fixed a bench and duckboards and rigged up an electric wire with occasional light bulbs. The tunnel was dimly white but the chalk walls and ceiling dripped. Our feet were wet and if we leaned against the wall our cloaks got sodden. It was difficult for anyone to get past once we were sitting in line. We were stuck, safe only from bombs.

The staff tried to divert our attention away from the cold and wet, so we practised passing messages. We called it Russian scandal, and we loved it. Before entering we had taken care to be next to the right person and well away from a member of staff to whom we could not possibly relay the message which arrived amid gales of giggles, horribly adulterated. Thank heaven it was soon decided that pneumonia was more likely to kill us than a bomb and the tunnel was abandoned.

The air-raid siren at night brought a procession of girls and staff downstairs, clutching torches and eiderdowns. We lay on the stone floor, glad of the carpet down the passage. When the All Clear sounded, usually at the coldest moment of the small hours, we groaned and trailed upstairs to cold beds and icy hot-water bottles. The dormitories were unheated, as in other schools, and we had a bath twice a week. As fuel was tightly rationed, a black line was painted at the four-inch level in the bath but this wasn't deep enough to warm us up. We filled hot-water bottles from the tap, hoping for a decent sleep before the wretched siren woke us. When it did, we pulled on warm clothes and went downstairs discussing hot-water bottles; to enjoy their last glimmers of warmth or leave them upstairs? The problem was insoluble. Rosemary summed it up, "Hottie is a stupid word for This Thing."

At the end of the spring term of 1942 Miss Crosthwaite, the headmistress, had some devastating news: the Americans needed WA as their headquarters. With our end-of-term reports came letters saying that WA had been requisitioned by the War Office. The Council had looked at alternative sites but found none to which WA might be evacuated. After nearly three years of war, the only available premises needed vast expenditure to equip them for our numbers. WA must close for the duration.

The 80 girls taking public examinations were offered temporary accommodation with a few WA staff at Headington School. I was taking School Certificate so this was accepted for me. The few WA staff who came to Headington proved their versatility during the few weeks before our exams. Miss Reynolds, a lively-minded Classicist, taught us six different subjects that summer term.

Our parents felt it important that while so much was changing we should be with our friends. Two of mine were aiming for Cambridge, and St Leonard's in Scotland was thought to provide good preparation. The distance was daunting but as some St Leonard's girls had earlier been removed overseas, there was room for 50 of us and several WA staff. Accordingly, a contingent boarded the train at Kings Cross, waved off by parents who would never normally have contemplated sending their daughters 400 miles to a school they had never seen and housemistresses they had never met.

Of course it was different from WA — much colder for a start, and no air-raids — but we had good teaching and good friends.

George Moore's form master in Cardiff was George Thomas, who was to become Speaker of the House of Commons:

When we moved to Cardiff I was sent to nearby Marlborough Road School, in the Roath area. My form master was George Thomas, who later became a Cardiff MP, Speaker of the House of Commons, and was finally elevated to the House of Lords as Lord Tonypandy. The impact of this unique man remains with me to this day. He used to come to school daily, by train, from Tonypandy and always wore a white shirt with a stiff collar, black jacket and black striped trousers. He taught us well, was strict but very fair, and he was highly respected by all of his pupils.

After a long absence from school through illness I returned in January 1941, but a few days later Marlborough Road School was destroyed by a 500-lb bomb. This led to another two weeks away from education, until alternative accommodation was arranged for our

52

class, with Mr Thomas, at a nearby school. Next to it was a bakery, where we could buy large hot buns for a penny before morning class.

One master at that time, Mr Horton, taught a class of boys who had failed to get to secondary education and remained in their first school until they reached the age of 14, when they could leave to start work. Mr Horton was a short man who taught by shouting from first thing in the morning until school ended in the afternoon. He always wore his trilby hat in class with the blackboard duster in the ridge on the top of the hat and sticks of chalk around the brim. His cane was in his left hand, a piece of chalk in the right. Thus armed, he was able to impose immediate attention and discipline with the cane and missiles (chalk thrown, followed by blackboard duster). One thing was certain, all boys behaved, listened and learned. No boy left school unable to read or write.

In September 1941 I proceeded to secondary education, boarding at Colston's School in Bristol. The fees were £21 a term. It was a shock to the system: damp underground shelters, appalling food, rigid discipline and regular beatings. In addition, we were taught by elderly masters, most of whom should have retired but stayed on because younger men had been called into the Forces. We also had lady teachers, most unusual in a boys' school at that time. Out of all of this came a sound education; the learning process was not lost because of the difficult circumstances.

All events of the war were followed with close interest by the boys at school. Many had fathers serving in the Forces. Sometimes it was reported that one had been killed in action. This had a sobering influence for a short while on everyone. Other boys had fathers who were taken prisoner. Although they were relatively safe, if in German custody, it still meant they would not be seen or their important influence felt until after the end of the war.

After the victory at El Alamein, church bells were rung for the first time in over two years to mark the event. On the Sunday concerned virtually the whole school stood watching the spire of Stapleton church, listening to the peals.

On occasion our sleep was disturbed by raid alerts. We then trooped in a well-drilled but dazed state, carrying our bedding, to the shelters where we remained until the All Clear. There was little enemy action after 1942, so the alerts were more of a nuisance than damaging. There was one nasty incident in August 1942, however. During the morning rush-hour a high-flying German plane dropped one bomb. It hit the ground in the middle of the city, destroying three crowded buses. Over 30 people were killed and another 30 badly injured. One of these was a boy from school who had a smashed leg. He was away from school for some time and when he returned he was on crutches, then had to use a walking stick for a long while. He was a constant reminder that the war was only just around the corner.

We were given two days off for VE Day in May 1945 and could go home but had to return to school each evening. We were permitted to bring our bikes so that we could get home the following morning. My father also got leave and managed to hitch-hike home from the airfield in Rutland where he was serving. When back at school in the evening I went with other boys for my first visit to a nearby pub and had my first pint of bitter, costing 1*s* 3*d*. All bounds and rules were broken and the situation ignored by "authority".

VJ Day was celebrated in August at home, with even more enthusiasm.

When I returned to school in September 1945 I found new, younger masters, more inspired teaching, better food and more sport. Peace certainly brought many changes for the better, including the first bananas for six years. All of this helped us to face that important cloud on the horizon — School Certificate!

The year 1947 began with trains grinding to a halt in vast snow drifts; colliers could not sail from the north-east ports to the Thames, and roads were blocked. The outcome was a vast fuel shortage, so no heating, light or power. When we returned to school we found the main boiler had burst. There was no possibility of repair so we lived by day in the still-warm classroom block and shivered when in other parts of the school. In addition there were no games. The cold, nasty conditions continued for nearly the whole term. It all ended when we were sent home four days early due to an outbreak of measles. I developed it in the middle of the holidays, when I had to spend a few days in bed.

In summer 1947 I sat the School Certificate examination. I achieved reasonable results, but not matriculation. To pass in those days you had to obtain credits in five specified subjects, including English, maths and a foreign language. Languages were not my forte, so no matric. That meant I was not eligible to proceed to the sixth form. So I put my school days behind me, probably much to the relief of my father, who had been demobbed in October 1945.

The fees had risen to £100 per annum and were about to rise to £120. This would have been a strain on his income, which I found out years later was about £600 at that time.

Gill Meason went to Christ's Hospital, Hertford, in September 1940. This school was founded, together with the boys' school now at Horsham, by King Edward VI and is the oldest girls' school in Britain:

I was nearly 11 when my mother accompanied me to Christ's Hospital. After various formalities we were taken to my house (Ward 6) and immediately to the wardrobe room, where I was required to strip and dress entirely in school clothes. My home clothes were packed in a small suitcase, in which I had brought the only things that we were required (and allowed) to bring:
    1 suspender belt
    1 pair bedroom slippers
    1 pair house shoes
    1 pair plimsolls
    Sponge bag
    Brush and comb
    Bible
    Writing case with paper and envelopes
    Pencil case
We were not allowed a wristwatch or fountain pen until we were in the Upper Fifth, when we might need them for public examinations.
    A modest amount of tuck was allowed, which was

locked up in a cupboard and issued by the Monitress on Wednesday, Saturday and Sunday afternoons.

My mother then left with my clothes and I was taken by my "school mother" to the dayroom. She was a very kind 5th former called Ann, who was a great support and mentor for three years. She helped me with my mending and comforted me in times of trouble. We each had to mend our own stockings, etc.

A girl of my age, Rosemary, who had been at the school for some time, offered to look after me and I soon felt at home. Unfortunately this was the start of the Battle of Britain and about half an hour after we were in bed I experienced my first air-raid. Within the next few weeks, it was decided we should sleep in the cellar, first on mattresses on the floor, then on specially built three-tier bunks. Although the cellar was stuffy and crowded, we felt safe and usually slept well.

Life was very structured. A whistle was blown to wake us at 6.50 a.m. We had to fill a jug with hot water and a mug with cold water, then return to our cubicles, draw the curtains, wash, clean our teeth, dress, empty our water, strip beds, fold blankets, and fold curtains. Then downstairs to do our hair (all fighting for two mirrors) in time for prayers at 7.20. Then we had to do our allocated household duties until 7.50, line up in the entrance hall in form order ready for "running round the Square", followed by marching up to breakfast.

At 8.40 a.m. there were back-drill or flat-feet exercises in the gym for those who were deemed to need it. As I was very small, I was also expected to hang for several minutes from the ribstalls to help me grow. I always marvelled that I didn't end up with ape-like arms.

At 9 a.m. we lined up in our caps and coats to walk to chapel, followed immediately by two lessons, break, and two more lessons. At 12.40, if we were not in the table-laying brigade, we had a few minutes free until lunch.

In winter after lunch we had organised games, music practice or, in bad weather, country dancing, which we loved. Then we had lessons from 4 to 5.30 p.m., followed again by the possibility of 15 minutes free before tea. In summer, we had lessons first and then games. Tea was followed immediately by prayers and then we had supervised prep until 7.45, which was bedtime for the juniors.

Our only really free time was on Saturday and Sunday evenings, between prayers and bedtime, but often at that time we needed to do our school needlework, which had to be completed by a certain date each term. We were always delighted when it rained on Saturday or Sunday afternoons, which meant we had extra free time instead of having to go for walks in crocodiles.

Sometimes on fine Saturdays we had "Ward games", when tolerant senior girls would organise communal games like Lurky or Grandmother's Footsteps, and sometimes on Saturday evenings they arranged indoor games. We used to make up entertainments, which we wrote and rehearsed for special occasions like our housemistress's birthday. Spring term evenings were often occupied practising for the singing competition — the whole Ward had to take part and we had to sing a Psalm and a prescribed song. This was a real chore as it ate into our precious free time.

Even during the war the buildings were usually

pleasantly warm. However, in cold weather when we had a few free minutes in Ward we liked to bag a radiator. Two of us would sit on the flat grid top, with our feet on a chair. Another two might sit on chairs hugging the pipes that led into the radiator, as we read or revised or gossiped.

We changed our blouses, stockings and blue knickers only once a week, and our white, calico knicker-linings twice a week. If we had colds, we could apply for old extra hankies, but also we used to wash them in the cloakroom basins and wrap them round the hot-water pipes to dry, which they did in about half an hour, providing a lovely warm nest in which we could bury our red noses.

We had baths twice a week, but were allowed only four inches of water. There was a period when we had to share the water with another person, taking it in turns to go first.

The teaching staff expected a high standard of work, and they taught us to work quickly. In our supervised prep sessions we were required to change subjects after 20 minutes, so we had to learn to complete written work within the allotted time. This was valuable practice for examinations.

Most crimes were very minor and the punishments nominal. Forgetfulness or carelessness or talking at the wrong time resulted in an "Order Report"; disobedience or insolence attracted a "Disorder Report"; and bad work a "Classroom" which was, in fact, a Saturday afternoon detention for the work to be redone. The worst part about these black marks was that on Friday nights, after prayers, any reports issued had to be publicly confessed. The Ward Monitress would ask "Are there any reports?", and the sinners would stand up and, in turn, say the nature of the report and the reason for it. A severe rebuke was then expressed but, if the crime were felt to be particularly heinous, or if one person had a series of reports, then they might be summoned to the study to experience a Study Blowing Up, after which the recipient would emerge in floods of tears. Reports were given only by teaching staff. Within the Ward, other sanctions were issued such as missing treats or being sent to bed early, or having extra tasks to do. I was once sent to sleep alone in the cellar because I visited a friend in the other dormitory with only my towel wrapped round me. I'd been anxious to deliver a message before having my bath.

Once I was in the sixth form life became somewhat more relaxed. With more time for private study, it was possible to fit in more reading for pleasure, and life was slightly less structured, though responsibilities increased. Eventually, I was promoted to the study and there were cosy evenings by the fire, making toast and tea. In my case, this coincided with the end of the war, which made everything extra pleasurable.

Ian Sandeman enjoyed life at his public school, including the compulsory Junior Training Corps:

My brother was six years older than me and joined the Royal Navy a few months before the war began. Soon after war was declared he went off to join his first ship "to fight the war in earnest". We are grateful to God that he came through the war unharmed.

I was at Norwood Preparatory School in Exeter until

1941 and then at King's School, Bruton, until the end of the war, and suffered no direct enemy action. The headmaster of Norwood School was a rather austere character, but I believe he ran the school well and it certainly achieved many good academic successes, with scholarships to well-known public schools. He was not averse to using the cane, but only when necessary, and none of us had a problem about this — except perhaps the one who was the culprit. (I usually managed to avoid this punishment!) Classes were small, which of course contributed to the school's good results. Only one teacher was called up and we children were encouraged to write to him from time to time. After his departure the staff comprised male teachers who must have been exempt from military service, and some ladies.

I won a scholarship to King's, Bruton, and on going there found myself in an environment very different from that at Norwood School. I enjoyed my time there right from the start, making several friendships which have endured for more than 50 years.

During the war the school expanded from around 100 pupils when I arrived to more than 150 by 1945, and additional dormitory houses were bought to accommodate the extra boarders. There were only about ten day pupils. At boarding school, where catering for larger numbers made things easier, we were well fed, although the fare was plain, and we remained fit and healthy. Also at Bruton we were allowed to keep in our lockers our own stock of sugar and jam, part of our total rations, for use as we wished. Once a week we would put out our jars to receive about 3 oz sugar, and each month we received about 8 oz jam.

At Bruton we had much more freedom out of school hours than at Norwood School. We received pocket money of one shilling (5p) each week (on the school bill, of course) and were allowed to shop in the local village — for 20 minutes per day. We could also explore the countryside on foot or bicycle, sometimes ranging quite far afield with the permission of the housemaster.

Membership of the school's Junior Training Corps (Army) unit was compulsory, and we were all taught something of the infantryman's role. I achieved the rank of sergeant in charge of a platoon, but I never had the ability to become a member of the Corps bugle band.

During the build-up to D-Day an American armoured division was stationed in the area near the school. One day a pupil met one of the officers out walking who, after a friendly chat, introduced himself as the commanding general. After that the school had many formal and informal contacts with his officers and men until they went off to Normandy.

Anna Cunningham found that the impact of the war led to an upheaval in her family life, which was reflected in her schooling:

My father left Scotland to do vital war work in England and, when our house in Port Glasgow was bombed in 1940, my mother and I went to live in our holiday flat on the island of Cumbrae. The island school taught only to Form II and, as I was about to enter Form IV, I joined other children from Cumbrae and Arran who went to

Rothesay Academy, a co-educational school on the island of Bute, for our secondary education.

It was not possible to travel daily so I became a weekly boarder, living in various approved boarding houses. This was quite a shock to me, a somewhat spoiled only child, and I had to go through a painful period of adjustment. However, in the end I was invited by one of my classmates to live in her parents' boarding house, where I was very well looked after and had congenial company of my own age. There were five schoolchildren there and we supported each other at times of crisis and helped each other with homework.

Going home at weekends was a complicated business, involving two boat journeys and three buses. The Clyde could produce fierce storms and sea fogs, when the steamers could not sail. On one occasion we reached Fairlie only to be told that the steamer could not sail due to a snowstorm, but we regarded it as an adventure, particularly when the ship's crew fed us with dumpling. Afterwards we walked back to Largs where the police found us somewhere to sleep.

I had always done well at Port Glasgow High School without making much effort, but this changed dramatically at Rothesay Academy. My last few months in Form III had been interrupted by frequent air-raids, and my new school had a higher standard, so I found myself very nearly at the bottom of my class. Worse still, I had missed out on taking German, which they started in Form III, and found myself taking English and science on the higher level, French, history and mathematics on the lower level, and having to drop Latin. I was so unhappy that I begged my father to allow me to leave school which, luckily for me, he refused. Slowly I began to improve, was promoted to the upper French class and in the end I achieved a respectable Higher Leaving Certificate at the age of 16. I went on to the sixth form, where I took up Latin again, began German and studied higher history, with a teacher to myself, and higher mathematics "for the good of my soul", according to the rector (headmaster).

Looking back I realise that I had a happy time at Rothesay Academy, working hard and growing up in a rather conservative environment. The war did impinge on us, as a succession of troops were billeted on us at our boarding house and I fell in love (or thought I had) with a Canadian soldier. As a member of the Sea Cadets I was taught by a tough sergeant how to row a heavy makeshift lifeboat.

H. J. (Jim) West was still at school when the war began; it was soon to disrupt his further education:

I was 17 at the start of the Forties, studying Latin and Greek at Christ's Hospital, near Horsham in Sussex, in the hope of winning a scholarship to Oxford. In those days there were no Government grants for university education and a student had to find about £300 a year to see himself through the course. Most Oxford colleges had a few keenly contested scholarships on offer, worth up to £100 a year. If you did win a scholarship, the Christ's Hospital authorities would help to increase the amount through their long-established connection with charitable foundations in the City of London. During the whole of 1940 I submerged myself in Classical studies and was fortunate to be awarded a Classical scholarship by Keble College, Oxford.

The evacuation from Dunkirk in May 1940 and the imminent threat of a German invasion had a profound effect on our lives at school. A branch of the Home Guard was quickly formed and I found myself a corporal in charge of a section. Horsham was on the direct route for German night bombers attacking London, and one of our duties was to provide a night watch from the chapel tower against the chance of bombs landing on the school. We also operated patrols in the surrounding countryside whenever a rumour was reported of a German pilot having bailed out. I enjoyed my spell of duty in "Dad's Army", not least because at the end of our stint we received a pork pie and a mug of cocoa, often served by the headmaster's wife.

The Warden of Keble was keen that I should come up and take a wartime degree, which could be completed in a year. But the idea of going up to Oxford in wartime did not appeal to me and, by chance, soon after my scholarship award, an officer came to the school looking for volunteers to join the Indian Army. The proposal was that after a few months' training in England, we would be shipped out to an officer training unit in India. After a six-month course we would be given a commission and join an Indian or Gurkha regiment. This prospect appealed not only to myself but also to two friends, who had also gained scholarships to Oxford. We left school in April 1941.

War brought changes to many lives; Noreen Beaumont found she was no exception:

In January 1940, quite unexpectedly and at a few days' notice, I was placed as a boarder at the Convent of the Nativity in Eastbourne. This was a sudden decision on the part of my parents, who were separated by the outbreak of war. My school holidays had been prolonged from the previous summer as there had been no secondary education available for me where my mother was teaching in a village in Kent. She and her young pupils had been evacuated there from south-east London. My father had been sent to Harrogate from London by the Civil Service (General Post Office division).

I was 11, old enough to amuse myself observing village life throughout my first autumn away from the city. Now, for the first time, I was to sleep away from my mother. I shared a dormitory with six other girls and a nun. Every morning we rose and dressed in silence and attended Mass in the chapel before breakfast. At night we undressed in our curtained cubicles and washed in warm water we brought in a jug and emptied into a bucket, the whole action requiring some strength and skill, as the pottery bowl was shallow and heavy. The younger girls in "Holy Angels" dormitory on the top floor had only cold water and no curtains.

The only male to enter the convent was the visiting priest and, once, a bishop.

There were only six pupils in my class and I was very well taught. We could play in the garden and were taken out at weekends. We wore an attractive blue serge pinafore dress, with toning shirt and cardigan. On Sundays and special days we wore a similar outfit, but in cream or white with brown wool or cotton stockings.

In May 1940 we began to hear the booming of guns across the Channel, and soon afterwards we were woken by an air-raid warning. We descended the stairs with only a small light from the moonlit sky outside. The school electricity was switched off at night not, I was told, to comply with the blackout, but as a precaution against fire.

After more disturbed nights we packed our suitcases and travelled by coach to Abingdon, where all pupils slept for a week in a large hall with beds almost touching each other. We then moved into a Georgian house on the main street to have lessons and sleep. Our meals and leisure time were spent in a charming old house on the Oxford Road, Lacies Court. We eagerly explored the panelled halls and galleries, and strolled or played in the orchard and walled garden, while overworked staff moved and remade our beds.

One day meals were perfunctory and no lessons were given. The nuns, half of them French, were at continuous prayer in the chapel. The teachers were congregated near the wireless, listening to successive news bulletins. A classmate was crouching by the teachers' room, her face blotched with tears.

"My daddy's a major in France," she whispered, "and I don't know if he'll escape." The British Army was gathering at Dunkirk, retreating from the German advance.

Back with my mother in Kent, there was little opportunity to enjoy a country summer holiday, as aerial combat began overhead with the Battle of Britain.

We joined my father in Harrogate. Mother stayed to look after us, taking temporary leave from her employers, the London County Council. She had been teaching one of three classes (of which one was on the stage) in a village hall. I remember the echoes and the small, high-up windows — also the primitive toilets in the school-yard. To make tea she would boil a kettle on a paraffin heater.

Mother took a job at Pateley Bridge, a journey of about nine miles. She carried the paraffin heater with her on the bus, as she found the school in the Yorkshire Dales extremely cold. Later she returned to teach for the London County Council, where pay and conditions were better.

Meantime, I could not start school, or even go out, as I had no suitable clothing. My trunk from the boarding school took four months to catch up with me, as troop movements had priority. I greeted with unaccustomed pleasure the arrival of my navy-blue melton overcoat. The expensive blue serge tunics lasted me for the next five years. I never changed to the old-style brown pleated gym-slip worn at my next school, taking full advantage of the latitude allowed to evacuees.

In October 1940 I cycled to Harrogate Grammar School, which had doubled its numbers and many of the teachers had been recalled from retirement. One of our Latin teachers bore a foreign name and spoke with a foreign accent. She must have been a refugee from the Nazi tyranny and was tormented by some of the naughtier boys. Bored, I failed to respond openly to her enthusiasm for European literature and learning, which I shared in secret. Many years later we recognised each other on a boat returning from Ostend. I apologised for my discourteous behaviour and she said others had expressed similar regrets. She was kind enough to blame the unsettled conditions of wartime evacuation.

At the end of the war I rejoined my mother in London and finally attended Mary Datchelor Girls' School, for which I had been enrolled in 1939, before our dispersal to the countryside. The school was in a state of transition, reuniting those who had remained in London with those who had been away for as long as six years. I was at first puzzled when some girls began conversing in a South Wales accent — they were sharing a solidarity acquired in years spent away from their families.

Because of timetable difficulties I was obliged to change two of my main subjects and repeat the previous year in my third subject. This meant continuing in school uniform and following much the same rules as an 11-year-old, until three months after my 19th birthday.

We were worked hard and we responded to the challenge. I prepared for and passed scholarship and entrance exams to enter a degree course, acted as school games captain and was awarded certificates in netball and swimming.

CHAPTER
THREE

Further Education

Universities and colleges were even more devastated by the war than schools. Until 1941 some arts students were allowed to complete two years at university if they showed exceptional promise, but in December 1942 it was announced that all male arts students would be conscripted at 18. Only medical, dentistry, science and engineering students were permitted to complete their courses, unless they failed their examinations. Instead of the usual preponderance of men, the women soon outnumbered them at college. There were a few men who had failed to pass the medical, and some conscientious objectors were allowed to continue their studies if they were considered to be to the national advantage, but this in no way compensated for the many who had volunteered or been called up. However, the male under-graduates were augmented by RN and RAF cadets who were admitted to short courses of six months to increase certain skills.

Many university buildings were requisitioned early in the war and the faculties had to find accommodation elsewhere. The headquarters building of London University was taken over by the Ministry of Education, and the various colleges moved elsewhere: University College to Bangor and Aberystwyth, King's College to Bristol, Glasgow, Birmingham and Leeds, Bedford College and Queen Mary College to Cambridge. The London School of Economics was also evacuated to Cambridge, as were the London medical students and Chichester Theological College, leading to severe overcrowding in the city.

Fire was a constant hazard, so distinguished professors at Oxford and Cambridge found themselves learning how to use stirrup pumps and protect their irreplaceable premises in case of fire. Vacations were a special problem, so foreigners studying at the universities, who were exempt from military service and had no homes to go to, were enrolled as fire-fighters. Cambridge was not affected by air-raids as were Oxford and other universities.

In addition to their studies, concentrated into a shorter period, students had to do some war work such as rolling bandages for hospitals or making sandwiches for canteens, as well as fire-watching.

Many women's teacher training colleges had to join the evacuation from London and elsewhere and found themselves in unusual accommodation. The Froebel Educational Institute moved from Roehampton to Knebworth House, Hertfordshire, where the young women went from the luxury of sleeping in a fourposter bed to camp-beds crowded into the same room. The women hitch-hiked to attend lectures — not considered dangerous in those days.

Some men were able to complete a year at university before joining the Forces; others preferred to volunteer as soon as they reached the age of 18. When the war ended they were able to complete their courses, and many found that they benefited from being mature students. Younger women appreciated the influx of older men and the added stimulus they gave.

Audrey Dench much preferred life in the London blitz to being evacuated with her school to a "safe" area:

I returned to my home in London from Byfleet at the beginning of 1940. I could not decide what to do until I met someone who was at Regent Street Polytechnic in London, studying commerce (shorthand, typing, book-keeping, commercial law, etc.). I quickly applied and was accepted.

The students were a cosmopolitan lot. There were several Germans, a Polish refugee and various other foreigners. One weekend the Government decided to intern all Germans and any alien they thought a risk, and on the Monday morning all our German students had disappeared. I, for one, was disappointed as they were different from anyone I had been at school with before.

I continued with this course, learning to touch-type (we typed the alphabet to music), a skill which I never lost, and many other things which I have completely forgotten. Unfortunately the Battle of Britain started and I was scared about travelling up to town every day on my own (I was only 17) and, when I was offered a job locally, I could not refuse. I was not qualified for anything and so was employed as a clerk, doing figures and typing. I was sorry that I did not complete my education but at the time we never knew what would happen from one day to the next and just took things as they came.

When the war ended, men and women who had been denied the opportunity to begin or to complete further education could now do so. This led to a much richer mixture of students of different ages than was normal. Noreen Beaumont was among those who had the benefit of this:

In 1947 I came refreshed from enjoying village life in France to study the History of French Language and Literature at what is now University College, Southampton, a modern red brick building augmented by some wooden huts left over from Army use in the First World War.

Here the syllabus and exam papers were set and marked by staff of London University. I could have followed the same course at the women's college in London, for which

I had sat an exhausting entrance exam — but was not offered a place. A women's college in Oxford had said, as the result of another gruelling test, that I could join the following year, as current places were taken by older returning ex-service personnel. There were many of these among staff and students at Southampton, and their maturity and broader vision were a great asset to college life.

Those who had to subsist on a grant and those who had family to support were a somewhat deprived group financially. London County Council had awarded me a grant on my passing Higher School Certificate at Advanced Level with Distinction and I felt I deserved independence from my parents. It was a blow to learn that their combined salaries took us nearly above the limit and so I had honour but only pocket money from the LCC.

There were many female students, but the lecturers were all male. Lectures were sometimes rambling, incoherent or inaudible, and delivered at the wrong speed for the class, from which no comment or criticism were permitted. About 60 of us would sit silently scribbling while a lecturer, standing on a platform, could dictate notes gathered many years earlier.

There was some individual attention in the language classes, and our essays were returned and discussed on a one-to-one basis. A personal tutor was available, but I missed the close and constant supervision of my female tutors in the sixth form I had just left, as well as the support and friendly rivalry of my classmates. The seminar system was not introduced until the late Fifties.

The students in halls of residence had opportunities to

work together during the evening and at weekends: they also had access to dictionaries and reference books which were still in short supply, whereas I was in isolated lodgings some miles out of Southampton. The Students' Refectory, especially when crowded, ensured we mixed with members of other faculties while availing ourselves of the novelty of a self-service system. There were debates, societies and balls, from which I returned on my bicycle along dark country lanes.

Despite the inexperience of newly appointed staff and the inflexibility and heavy workload of the London external system, most students graduated successfully — but I had to accept that I would not be one of them, having been allotted as my second compulsory subject a language in which I was still at beginner's level. It was realised too late that I was never going to reach the required level in time.

Disheartened and wondering how I was going to face my future and, worse, my parents, I was only too glad to accept when my favourite lecturer, for whom I had always done my best work, made an unexpected offer of marriage. Students were not expected to marry during their course. Indeed, in 1956 a woman I knew who asked for leave of absence as she was "married and expecting a baby" was in danger of expulsion until two college wives interceded successfully for her retention.

In peacetime Britain imported much of its food and other necessities but during the war shipping was sunk at an alarming rate and it became essential for the country to produce more of its own food. So agriculture and horticulture became very important. Betty Matson studied for a BSc degree in horticulture:

In early 1940 I was accepted for a degree course in horticulture at Swanley Horticultural College in Kent. My father could not afford the full fees, but I was fortunate to be awarded scholarships from the college and from my school (Christ's Hospital), £120 from each, leaving my father another £120 or so to pay. When the term began in September the college had been evacuated to the Midland Agricultural College at Sutton Bonington, an outpost of Nottingham University. Here the staff and students had to "integrate" with those of MAC, which must have been more difficult for the Swanley staff (and Principal) than for the students, some of whom met their future partners there.

Horticulture had been well developed at Swanley, especially the decorative gardens and greenhouses, but at MAC the emphasis had been on agriculture and market-gardening. Some plant collections were brought up from Swanley but as it was wartime the main concern was food production. Flowerbeds round the buildings were sown with beet, carrots and parsley instead of asters, marigolds, etc. The parsley was cut and dried and sent to market.

The students helped to plant a new orchard in the spring of 1941, delayed until quite late in March owing to the long, cold winter. The space between the young trees was used to sow vegetables. As seed was in short supply, it was measured out for each row and if we ran out of seed before the end of the row we had to go back and pick some up!

We all had our turns of doing the floral decorations in the college buildings, stoking the greenhouse boilers, watering and ventilating the greenhouses. If there was a sudden storm we had to rush out and shut the glass "lights" over the frames, or on frosty nights cover them with matting or sacks. In the summer there was scarecrow duty in the strawberry field before breakfast — which we later discovered was to deter some of the locals from helping themselves!

All the horticulture students had to take a short course in either poultry-keeping or bee-keeping, and we all had lectures and practical work on surveying, carpentry, mechanics (of lawnmowers and tractors) and book-keeping, as well as chemistry and soil science, botany, plant pathology and the "principles and practice" of horticulture. We also kept detailed diaries and weather records.

Being some way from the village we made our own entertainment. There was country dancing, a choral club, a hop on Saturdays, plays and talks. We also organised our own sport and periodically supported the national campaigns for National Savings for Spitfires, submarines, etc., by dressing up and parading through the village. Although untroubled by enemy action at Sutton Bonington, we were kept awake on the night of the air-raid on Coventry, about 30 miles to the southwest.

In the summer vacation most students took jobs "on the land", some inspecting potato crops for disease, some working in market gardens or private gardens. I worked at Seabrook's fruit farm north of Chelmsford, living in digs (a thatched cottage) and being collected in a lorry for picking blackcurrants and plums. We were paid piece-rates and I soon learned to keep an eye on my pile of boxes at the end of the row.

In the summer of 1942, with invasion now unlikely, the college returned to its home in Hextable, Kent. Some of the students stayed at MAC at the end of term to help the Swanley staff pack and dispatch tools, apparatus, books and plants, but I and another student went in advance to Hextable to help other members of staff unpack and rearrange these items as they arrived. When term started we had Red Cross classes in First Aid, and the local firemen gave us instruction in dealing with incendiary bombs.

With food rationing, some mornings the main item for breakfast was Marmite on toast. But there was always porridge. In those days, the method used was to sprinkle the oats into boiling water and then simmer gently for about two hours, stirring from time to time. Gladys, the college cook, used to get up at 5 a.m. to do this, until she discovered that by heating it to boiling point the night before and putting it in a hay-box overnight she could have an extra hour in bed.

When it came to examinations, we had to do our practical horticulture at the RHS gardens at Wisley and the chemistry practical in London. Fortunately we all passed, gaining a BSc (Horticulture) as external students of London University in 1943. Eventually Swanley Horticultural College was amalgamated with the South-East Agricultural College to form Wye College, an outpost of London University.

Elizabeth Risius had to move many times during her studies at horticultural college:

I entered Swanley Horticultural College in September 1943 to study the theory and practice of horticulture for a diploma course (others took a more academic degree course). Our days were filled with lectures and with long hours of pruning fruit-trees, potato-picking, weeding vegetables and tending plant-houses. Our nights were punctuated with fire-watching duties, air-raid warnings and the distant drone of enemy planes. That was until the night of 1-2 March 1944, when we left our beds at 2 a.m. to gather reluctantly but obediently in the common-room of the main college house and the nearby farmhouse. Forty minutes later, several bombs, off-loaded by a departing bomber, fell across the college grounds, one landing beside the wall directly outside the common-room. The huge wooden shutters over the windows fell inwards, the lights went out, and there was a rattle of falling plaster and glass, then silence. Our head student was killed and another seriously injured; others sustained injuries that have dogged them all their lives. We retreated to the damp shelters in the vegetable gardens, fortified by Horlicks tablets, and I was one of those later taken down the road to a staff house. In the morning we had to walk through the village in dirty night-attire, watched by the local inhabitants. Our belongings were somehow collected, though it was considered unsafe to go upstairs, and we left in whatever we could find to cover our pyjamas, faces streaked with dust and carrying anything we could. My possessions were folded in an eiderdown.

79

As my home was in a defence area I always had to be met at King's Lynn station by my parents, who would assure the station authorities that I lived there and, of course, we had to show our identity cards. I can still see my mother's face when I stepped off the train after the bombing at Swanley: she was shocked that I was so dirty, inadequately clothed and clutching an eiderdown.

From that moment the organisation that went on behind the scenes must have been stupendous. The first-year degree students were sent to Royal Holloway College at Englefield Green in Surrey. I was among the diploma students who went to Hampshire Farm Institute at Sparsholt, near Winchester.

Our Swanley lecturers came in relays to instruct us, a month of botany with Mrs Reynolds, a month of plant pathology and entomology with Miss Schimmer, chemistry with Dr Smith (though I cannot recall there was a laboratory or any equipment), and horticulture with Miss Page and Miss Sanders. We worked at least an hour before breakfast, packing lettuce and leeks for market, but the Institute staff were very kind to us and gave us a lot of help and instruction.

We walked or cycled everywhere, up the hills surrounding Winchester, into the neighbouring woods, at that time filled with lily-of-the-valley and Solomon's Seal, towards Stockbridge where the US Army was stationed (the GIs were very friendly and I was even offered a life on a cherry farm in the States). D-Day arrived and the gliders came over, the roads were choked with Army vehicles, and the Americans departed. We certainly saw history in the making.

We were all reunited in the autumn in two large houses in the village of Ripley in Surrey: we were starting on a year at the RHS gardens at Wisley. How this was arranged we never knew and never asked, but in return for our labour at a time of acute staff shortages, we were given the use of the Society's buildings and facilities. We pruned the roses; weeded the rock garden; we planted trees and shrubs on Battleston Hill; staked the plants in the long herbaceous borders; and I recall cutting with handshears the hornbeam hedges that run behind those borders. We identified conifers in the arboretum with Mrs Reynolds; we potted up and on in the potting sheds. Lectures were held in the lecture theatre and we were given two attics as a common-room where we ate our packed lunches.

The winter that year was severe and much snow fell. Ripley Court was among the coldest places in the land, with even the hot-water bottles freezing in our beds. We had some compensation with skating on the pond in the grounds, but it was a relief when spring came, followed by the summer that brought VE Day. There were local celebrations in which we joined enthusiastically, but as we had two days' leave, some of us cycled the 30 odd miles to London. Some went to the Palace and shouted for the King; I went to the Mall; I also recall seeing the bonfires lit on top of Highgate Hill. And then we cycled back again.

Finally we moved to our fourth home in three years, Wye College. We were, by that time, third-year students, entering the last phase of our training before the exams. The college buildings were being repaired and refurbished after the wartime neglect and damage, and the quads were littered with baths, basins and piping.

81

We diploma students had rooms in the main quad or on the far side of the college. We ate in the dining-hall and the Principal intoned a Latin grace before and after the meal. We had lectures in rooms all over the college. As our numbers were gradually increased by an intake of male students (some school-leavers, some demobbed from the Forces, some returning to finish an interrupted course), we began to feel more of an integrated community, something which we had so lacked during the preceding years.

By January 1940, at the age of 19, Dick Cunningham was already half-way through his second year at Glasgow University, where he was studying for an Honours Degree in Classics. His course was interrupted by the war:

My subjects at university were Latin II, Greek II, and German. I had intended my third subject to be History II but, with the outbreak of war just four months previously, I decided to improve my German.

The severe black-out in the first term had reduced quite dramatically the number of evening meetings, but in the second term conditions improved and, projected suddenly to being treasurer of the Alexandrian (Classics) Society and even finding myself promoted to playing in the university's mixed doubles badminton team, I was kept occupied.

I left the Artillery section of the university's Officer Training Corps (OTC). Six months before the outbreak of war I had voluntarily appeared before a board and been accepted into the Army's Officer Cadet Reserve and had been given my Army number. This meant I would be called up on or near my 20th birthday and, as I saw my entrance to the Army looming, I saw no point in wasting my time in the OTC. I also did not work as hard at my classes as I should have done and, although I passed all subjects, I did not get the good marks and certificates of excellence that I had received in my first year. Fearing my physical fitness might not meet the Army's requirements, I left university at the end of the year and took six weeks of very arduous forestry work before being called up.

About the time of Germany's defeat in 1945 the Government announced that those who, before joining up, had had bursaries to universities (which were much rarer than they are nowadays), would be released in time to return to university in October 1945 to complete their degrees, irrespective of their demobilisation rating number. Being then stationed in the south of England, I went to my university on my next leave and asked that they apply for me to be demobilised in good time. I was released about the end of September but, after more than five years away from Classics, I could no longer face the grammar of those two languages and opted for an Honours Degree in History. Consequently, I found myself in History II, Junior Honours History and Constitutional Law and History. I was in a group of ex-servicemen of similar calibre to myself; we greatly enjoyed each other's company and most of us went for tea after an afternoon lecture. I re-joined the History Club at the professor's invitation and found myself both lecturing on my part in the Desert War and proposing the vote of thanks to a senior lecturer for his words of wisdom which, because of my age and intervening experience, I found no difficulty in criticising (to everyone's surprise) as well as praising. I resumed my sports which were somewhat rusty.

Approaching my 26th birthday I thought I should be looking for a job, so I went for various interviews in London. In February 1946 the Secretary of State for the Colonies offered me the post of Cadet in the Provincial Administration of Northern Rhodesia. I sailed for Cape Town in May, having missed two end-of-year examinations shortly beforehand. Two perturbed lecturers had reproached me for not writing the examinations. I replied that within a week I would be on the high seas and did not see the point. I learnt later that several other ex-servicemen had followed my lead and defaulted from university. The university agreed that students with a suitable number of subjects to their name would be granted a War Degree and so I was capped MA (no Honours) *in absentia* in January 1949.

The Government of Northern Rhodesia sent me for two terms in 1948-9 to Oxford University on what was called the Devonshire Second Course. There I was accepted by Balliol College, largely because one uncle had been their Snell Exhibitioner during part of the First World War. I concentrated on Tropical Agriculture and also enjoyed mixing with Colonial Service officers from many different colonies and different occupations. I refereed many rugby matches for the college, went weekly to the best seat in the dress circle of the Oxford Theatre, won the prize in the first-ever quiz held by the Oxford University Philatelic Society, and generally enjoyed myself.

Anna Cunningham was able to fulfil her ambition and achieve an Honours Degree at Glasgow University:

From my first year at university I knew that I wanted to concentrate on history, and in those happy days did not concern myself with choosing a vocational degree. My history professor once told the class that he thought history was an excellent training for life, enabling one to examine the facts and come to a conclusion based on them.

I was the first of my mother's and father's families to enter university and was well aware of the privilege I enjoyed in doing so. My parents were not affluent and for them it was a sacrifice to put me through university. Staying in residence was too expensive and so I travelled daily by train the 20 miles to Glasgow. The Carnegie Trust helped students to pay their fees on condition that they passed their exams. I had the Trust's help from 1944 to 1948. In my final year Renfrewshire County Council gave me a generous grant, and I also worked during my vacations.

Because an MA Honours Degree, if unsuccessful, could only be repeated after ten years, I decided to combine an Ordinary MA, including the seven liberal arts, with an MA Honours Degree. This meant a very full curriculum. In several subjects I managed to do well enough to obtain an exemption from writing the final examination. This applied to geology, and all I had to do were the practical examinations: identifying rocks and fossils, and making a contour map. I was lucky that a kind invigilator pointed out to me that my contour map, nicely coloured, had mountains instead of valleys! I just had time to redo it. At least by the end of my third year I had a degree to my name and could proceed to Senior Honours History with a feeling of something achieved.

University life was not all hard work and no play. I took part in community singing, joined the Scottish Nationalist and History clubs and, on occasion, danced the afternoons and nights away.

I did achieve a second-class pass in Honours History, which was a fair reward for the years of studying and the trauma of examinations, not to mention the anxiety caused by having to read aloud my Honours dissertation. This latter led me to faint into the lecturer's arms. My classmates teased me that it was the reason for the good mark I obtained!

Gill Meason gained a place at Lady Margaret Hall, Oxford:

In October 1948 I began my university course, studying French. Although Oxford was my home town, I lived in college and, having been at boarding school for eight years, it was lovely to be based in Oxford. To me, university life seemed perfection. I rapidly made half a dozen good friends and the timetable of lectures and tutorials was enough to give structure to the week, while leaving ample time to enjoy the freedom.

I was keen on drama and joined the Experimental Theatre Club. If we wished to perform in a play, we had to apply for "Acting Leave". This would normally be granted only twice a year, so we had to make do with taking on other jobs like "call boy", scene shifter, or prompter, which of course used just as much time.

Men and women were not allowed in each other's colleges before midday or after 8 p.m. However, by wearing our academic gown and carrying books, we could walk purposefully past the porter as though going to a tutorial and call on friends for morning coffee, feeling very wicked.

This was an unusual time at universities because male students might be boys of 18, straight from school, men in their early twenties who had served two years of National Service, or mature men of any age who had served in the Forces during the war.

In 1945 Jim West was released from the army, so he was able to begin to study for a degree at Keble College, Oxford, the following October:

I was one of the returning servicemen who formed the majority of undergraduates at Oxford during the first post-war years. Most of us found it difficult to settle down to academic studies to begin with, but we were generally a more serious and sober intake than the "Brideshead" generation of the inter-war years.

I had decided to move away from the Classics and to take politics, philosophy and economics instead. My philosophy tutor, Donald MacKinnon, later to become Professor of Divinity at Cambridge, was a brilliant but eccentric don, who had the disconcerting habit of

87

scratching the palm of his hand with a razor blade while listening to the weekly essay. He was a very stimulating teacher, patient and tolerant of my seeming inability to grasp the fundamentals of the subject. My economics tutor, E. M. Hugh-Jones, was much more down to earth, having spent the war in the Ministry of Food.

Keble College had been handed over to the Ministry of Defence during the war and had only just reverted to college status when I went up in October 1945. There was therefore no experience of college life for any of us to draw upon. Societies and college teams had to be organised from scratch and there was a certain reluctance among many of the ex-servicemen to volunteer. But slowly college life took on its normal course and the first all-night summer ball, held in the quad in June 1946, was considered an outstanding success.

Oxford in those immediate post-war years was an example of triumph over austerity. Food rationing remained at its wartime level and coal was in very short supply. A coal fire was the only source of heat in our rooms at Keble and we were rationed to one bucket of coal a week. But these were small hardships compared with the experiences many had had during the war. We were glad to be alive and able to enjoy Oxford at peace. At least there was plenty of beer; the most a restaurant could charge for a meal was five shillings (25p); and most of the returning servicemen had accumulated pay and gratuities to spend, as well as being provided with Government grants to meet tutorial and living expenses. If the winter of 1946-7 was the coldest of the century, it was followed by a glorious summer. It was a good time for poling a punt down the Cherwell, bathing in Parsons Pleasure and watching the great New Zealand left-hander, Martin Donelly, scoring centuries for the Varsity cricket team in the Parks.

In my last year I had to get down to serious hard work, with final exams in view, and to decide what to do after I had graduated. As a student of economics I was interested in a career in business and applied for a management traineeship with Unilever. I was lucky enough to be accepted, joined Unilever in September 1948, and remained with that company for the rest of my working life.

CHAPTER
FOUR

Employment

The unemployed of the Thirties were soon to find work during the Forties, or they were conscripted into the Forces. Only a few male conscientious objectors, the elderly and those who did not pass the medical were exempt or allowed to work in non-essential jobs. Women, too, between 18½ and 50 were conscripted; only those with small children being exempt. Child care was provided so that mothers with children under 14 could be employed if they wished, and one in seven did so.

This opened up a whole new world for many women who had not worked since they were married and others who had never worked at all. The wealthy had to learn to do without their servants, some learning to cook for the first time. Teachers and other professional women who had had to give up work on marriage were now encouraged to return to work to take the place of men who had been called up, and older men came out of retirement to join them. Nurses in particular were in great demand.

Unskilled women were drafted into factories, including aircraft and munitions factories, where the demand was intense. Many of them undertook men's jobs that would have been considered completely outside their capabilities in peacetime. Hours were long, many working an 80-hour week; some in the aircraft industry worked seven ten-hour days a week in appalling conditions. Because of the black-out ventilation was poor, and the noise of machinery deafening.

Churchill had been appointed Prime Minister on 10 May 1940 and headed an all-party National Government. Ernest Bevin was a very successful Minister of Labour. In the early days of the war so many miners had been allowed to enlist that the workforce was seriously depleted. Coal was an essential commodity, so from the end of 1943 10 per cent of all men reaching military service age were chosen by ballot to become miners. They were called "Bevin Boys": it was a very unpopular service and men from all social classes were conscripted.

Parliament was dissolved early in the summer of 1945 and a landslide victory for Labour followed. Among other things they proposed increased nationalisation of industry and an extension of the welfare state. In 1948 the National Service Act required all 18-year-old men to undertake a compulsory two-year period of military service, so that there would be a nucleus of trained men available should war break out again. The discipline imposed was considered beneficial to the youth of the nation, although many objected to it.

Men returning from the Forces often found it very difficult to fit into civilian life, especially if they had no work. The Resettlement Advice Handbook, issued by the Ministry of Labour, was mainly to help people find employment, but many of them had psychological problems that were more urgent. In some cases civilians who had been exposed to endless air-raids had had a harder time than their menfolk, and husbands and wives could not settle down together after a long separation.

When they were demobbed, men and women were given a civilian suit, overcoat and underwear, also a small gratuity according to rank and length of service. Those who had been in work before being called up expected to have their old jobs back, but they had been replaced by others who had gained seniority by length of service. Many were not prepared, after all their battle experience, to accept a junior post. Some emigrated to the Commonwealth countries, where they were promised greater opportunities, but others led frustrated lives.

Louis Quinain was a country policeman during the war:

When the war began, I was a young policeman shortly to be married. In March 1940 I was moved from a town to a country beat, just outside Guildford. It was not deep country, for the village was known as a "stockbrokers' dormitory", and slept ten millionaires.

It was here, among a mixture of high and low society, that my wife and I took over a house provided by the Police authority, effectively the village police station. Wages were £3 10*s* (£3.50) a week, plus a house in which we lived rent- and rate-free. Since we were the only two occupants it meant that, while I was out on patrol, my wife had to answer the telephone, take messages from headquarters and attend to callers at the door. She was, virtually, an unpaid, unofficial policewoman. All of my patrolling was done on a bicycle, eight hours in twenty-four, some by day, some by night, on a beat stretching ten miles from end to end. Road accidents were infrequent since most of the beat was not on a main road, and petrol rationing severely restricted the use of cars.

During the early years of the war, when our cities were suffering severe aerial bombing, I would be called on to join police reinforcements drafted to a bombed area in another police district, always provincial, not metropolitan. Among my worst experiences here was the Southampton blitz, where the bombed remains of the old Spitfire works (already evacuated to a country area) were now a wasteland of rubble and twisted metal alongside the docks.

Then came the Police call-up. Until 1940 all policemen were in a reserved occupation, meaning that none was subject to call-up to serve in the Armed Forces, but now all men under 25 on a certain date were enlisted. I was just over 25 and so remained on the beat.

Jobs on a country beat were many and varied, increased by wartime restrictions and regulations. Enforcing the

93

black-out when air-raid wardens were not around, and immobilisation of stationary cars were two of the most common, the latter as a precaution against a sudden invasion by enemy troops, fully expected in 1940 after Dunkirk. To this end all villages had their own "Invasion Committee" to co-ordinate the arrangements in the area and with neighbouring villages. It was presided over by the local LDV (Home Guard) Commander, and consisted of the local constable, ARP wardens and special constables (unpaid part-timers). After Dunkirk we met every week, expecting action any moment, when the church bells would ring.

Later on, during enemy night bombing, as our defences improved, several bombers were shot down in the area by our night-fighter planes. I went to a plane crash very early one morning, when the dawn eventually revealed the pilot spread-eagled, and dead, high in a tree, his parachute tangled in the branches. His plane had exploded on landing, blowing the rest of his crew to the four winds. It was a sombre business collecting bits of bodies into a bag.

When it became evident that Germany would eventually lose the war, with the Allied armies advancing into Europe after D-Day, the invasion precautions were eased and, in time, cancelled altogether. By this time my work was becoming less geared to wartime demands and more towards routine duties, like visiting farms to sign the "animal movements' register", and jobs related to the Diseases of Animals Act. Other jobs would arise from items in the daily news and crime bulletin, issued by headquarters. There was always lost and found property to be dealt with,

also the occasional misdemeanour by schoolchildren —
usually the evacuee schools from London.

Edith Rolfe's career followed her training at
horticultural college:

After graduating from horticultural college I took up a post
as "lady gardener" at Wycombe Abbey School in Buck-
inghamshire. My job lasted only nine months, as the
American High Command took over the premises. Queen
Anne's School, Caversham, approached me to work at the
school under the head gardener, whose son had been
called up, and I accepted. Other men working there were
called up: two Land Army girls were brought in and I was
asked to keep an eye on them to try and help the head
gardener accept women as employees. This took some
diplomacy! I was there for three years and got on very well
with the head gardener and his wife, and tried to ease the
blow when their son was killed in Italy.

I left to take a teaching post in a secondary modern
girls' school in Didcot. There were two acres of land that
had been used for growing potatoes and left in a very
rough state. I was able to make an attractive school garden,
teaching biology (horticulturally biased), and a few other
subjects. I remained there for the rest of the war and in fact
stayed 11 years. The children grew vegetables, fruit and
flowers, and there were close links with the domestic
science department, so they experienced crops from seed
to harvest to the table.

Dennis Thompson's working life was affected by the war and its aftermath:

I was 19 at the start of the Forties and worked in the production and planning office of an electrical and mechanical engineering firm in Acton, cycling the six or so miles to and from Southall morning and evening. Usually the air-raids had ended by the morning but in the dark winter months of 1940 they began at 5 p.m. We cyclists were able to dodge the police and air-raid wardens, who endeavoured to clear the main roads of people during a raid by sending them to shelters. We cycled along the parallel back streets. Seeing well-known buildings and dwelling houses wrecked by bombs was shocking at first but, as with all things, we got used to it.

Day-time air-raids in the vicinity of work caused much interruption at first, as all the staff had to go to the underground shelter, but loss of production caused a rapid rethink. As a result, it was only on the receipt of a red alert (bombers overhead) that personnel dived under desks or machines, or went down to the shelter, if nearby. We hoped for the best.

My subsequent war service took up a large slice of my young life. When I was demobilised my old post was not available and I was offered a different job, still associated with production but in the diesel engineering department, so there was new terminology, drawings and parts to assimilate.

In 1948 I married Pauline, in Yorkshire, and then we had the problem of finding our own home. We were fortunate as, at the end of the decade, after living with my parents for a short while, we moved to Yorkshire where I obtained a job in the finance office of the National Coal Board. Again we spent only a short time with Pauline's parents before buying a small terrace house, and our life together really began.

In common with many ex-service personnel, Audrey Dench found it hard to adjust to civilian work:

After my war service in the WRNS I went back to my old office job, but I hated it. Stuck in an office with ladies who had hardly been any further than Wandsworth, we demobbed people felt suffocated, undervalued and unable to stick the petty behaviour and uninspiring conversation of the old hands. I had had three years on an airfield doing all sorts of different things and travelling to interesting places, and to return to this restricted and confining life was more than I could bear. In the end I took myself off for a while and eventually returned to London just after the Health Service started.

I got myself a job with a local dispensing optician as receptionist doing, apart from reception work, typing, writing out orders, accounts, and making the tea, of course. I really did enjoy that job. We were extremely busy as everyone wanted to jump on the free bandwagon. Spectacles were prescribed for many people who did not really need them as well for those who did. We were inundated with work, so much so that I used to go to bed at night and write out orders for lenses in the comfort and peace of my bedroom! Everyone went mad like this in all departments of the Health Service. After a while I realised that, if I stayed, I would be doing all the same things for the rest of my working life. In the end, I applied to do teaching and was accepted at an emergency training college in Peterborough in 1950.

When the war ended, many of us went off in new directions and the old habit of living and schooling in one area, working there, marrying and staying there became a thing of the past.

Ivy Page describes the unusual career of her late husband as well as her own employment during the Forties:

My husband, Eric W. Page, was born partially blind. Nonetheless, he volunteered for the Armed Forces in July 1940, after Dunkirk, when the Army had been seriously depleted. Eric, who had led a normal life and concealed his sight impairment, joined the Pioneer Corps, which consisted of men not 100 per cent fit.

On 27 September 1940, under the threat of a German invasion, Eric's regiment was posted to Selsey Bill on the Sussex coast and he and two other men were each given a rifle, with one round of ammunition. Although none of them had ever fired a rifle before, they were given a strategic bridge to guard. Of these three, one man was doubled up with a hernia and could not stand up straight, the second was as deaf as a post — the other two had to signal to him when the guns were firing — and Eric's sight was too bad for him to tell friend from foe! After a while he was recommended for promotion, but when he came before the Medical Board they discovered his sight deficiency, and he was immediately discharged from the Army.

Eric was aware that there were plenty of jobs in industry that blind people could do. Hitherto the blind had only worked in sheltered workshops, doing shoe repairs, piano tuning and basketwork. Their wages were subsidised.

A friend suggested that Eric should contact the Royal National Institute for the Blind with his ideas, and as a result he was taken on their staff as the first placement officer for the blind. With his inventive mind, Eric designed a micrometer with a Braille scale, using meccano for the prototype, which a Liverpool firm took up. As a result, many blind people were engaged in inspection work in factories measuring to ten thousandths of an inch. From there he got people employed mostly in banks as telephone switchboard operators, using the old push plug system; then to typing and audio-typing; and gradually opened the field in many occupations. During that period an Act of Parliament was passed making it obligatory for a percentage of disabled people to be employed by firms. For the first time the blind were able to earn a proper wage.

In 1937 I had obtained a post with the British Metal Corporation in Gresham Street, London. They were going over to mechanised accounts, an innovation in those days. By 1939 I was in charge of the whole installation of Power Samas machines, a system that was the forerunner of computers.

In 1940, when first one European country and then

another fell to the Germans, I would go to church of a Sunday evening and sing, with many of the congregation in tears, the National Anthem of the latest country to to be taken over. When France fell we tried to sing the Marseillaise, with almost everyone in tears.

In July 1944, when the flying bombs and rockets were being used against England, I evacuated from Harrow to Mochdre, near Colwyn Bay. With a child of two and a baby of three months I travelled with a large bassinet pram filled with the babies and what few possessions I could manage (mostly baby things). Our journey took twelve hours, and when we arrived in Mochdre it was like another world. The people were quite oblivious to the war!

The need to replace staff who had been called up led to Grace Horseman becoming a personnel officer:

My job as secretary to the Managing Director, Mr Fisher, and to the Company Secretary, Mr Barwell, of May & Baker changed completely in 1940. My predecessor, among other things, had been responsible for recruiting staff, a fairly rare occurrence in peacetime, with a representative from the appropriate department making the final choice. Once war was declared many of the young chemists at the company's pharmaceutical section and office staff, who belonged to the Army, Navy and Air Force reserves, were called up and had to be replaced urgently. Sadly, a large proportion of them, especially Air Force crews, were killed in the Battle of Britain. Much of my time was spent searching for and interviewing replacements, so much so that Mr Fisher complained that he could never find me when he wanted me. When I explained the position, he asked me to engage another secretary for himself and Mr Barwell, whilst I concentrated mostly on personnel work.

I realised my lack of specialised training and joined the Industrial Welfare Society. Later in 1940 I heard that the Government recognised the importance of having trained personnel officers at every factory, so they were running a trial course at the London School of Economics, evacuated to Cambridge. On the recommendation of the Welfare Society I applied and was accepted.

When I had qualified I was offered a post as assistant personnel officer at W. D. & H. O. Wills's Bedminster factory. Olga Spicer was in charge of the Personnel Department at Bedminster, with Miss Wilkerson head of all the cigarette and tobacco factories' personnel officers. Olga was an excellent person to introduce me to work in a factory. Wills had a long-standing welfare policy, with many facilities for employees. Also, Olga considered it essential that every member of the personnel department should experience at first hand all the different kinds of work the factory employees were asked to undertake.

Cigarettes were an important morale-booster to the troops, and demand was great. My fiancé, Ken, was a prisoner-of-war in Italy and Germany, and from time to time the Red Cross would supply cigarettes as well as food in their parcels. He was a non-smoker and in the early days fellow prisoners would exchange chocolate for his cigarettes, but eventually food became so short that no one

101

was prepared to do a swop. He found that smoking reduced the hunger pangs, and so unfortunately developed the habit. Later he preferred a pipe.

Although I enjoyed being part of a team, after two years there I felt I should move to a smaller factory where I would be in charge, and went to G. N. Haden & Son at Trowbridge, Wiltshire. This was a well-established heating engineering firm and very different, as they were doing work for the Admiralty. I was responsible for engaging and looking after office staff as well as factory employees, day and night staff.

As with other industries, many of the men had been called up, and girls who were conscripted and had opted for factory work were directed to Hadens. Many came from Cornwall and elsewhere, and were billeted on the local people. There was a strong social club and I was much involved in organising entertainments and other activities. Many American as well as British men from the Forces were stationed in the area, more and more so as D-Day approached. As they were away from home they appreciated being invited to dances and social evenings, and the girls were grateful to have partners. I also introduced the employees to rambling and cycling tours, and we ran a flower show.

Then Hadens at Trowbridge were taken over by another company, who wanted me to act as welfare officer for both branches, but I declined as I preferred the personnel side of the work. So I sought a post in London to be with my parents. Doodlebugs (V1) and later V2s were presenting a renewed threat to the capital and I wanted to be with them. I was accepted by Allen & Hanbury as personnel officer at their Bethnal Green factory.

They, too, produced pharmaceutical products. Penicillin was being developed and I was shown that department when I toured their Ware factory.

There was a very friendly relationship with directors, doctors and staff, but I gave Mr Hanbury a nasty shock when the time came for me to leave in February 1946. When I went to say goodbye to him he asked why I was leaving. I said I was going to have a baby and he looked most embarrassed. He had not heard that Ken and I had married in June 1945, after his release from POW camp in Germany. To avoid confusion I had kept my maiden name of Solkhon. I hope someone disillusioned him later!

Doris Maguire worked near High Wycombe during much of the war:

At the outbreak of war I was working as a mother's help in the family of a local businessman, who owned a large farm near High Wycombe. There were five daughters, and I was treated as one of the family. There was no need for me to be transferred to war work, as helping out on the farm at haymaking, feeding animals and collecting and grading eggs was considered to be a reserved occupation.

However, as time went by I felt I should be doing more, so with an older girl I applied to join the WAAF. We passed the medical and had to submit our birth certificates; as I was six months short of the regulation joining age of $17^1/2$ that fell through.

Then I worked as a nursery nurse in a day nursery, set up for mothers working in the factories. The hours were long and the journeys difficult, as the buses were not reliable. So I was sent for a job at Hoover's aircraft factory in High Wycombe. After passing a medical and eye test, I was placed in a machine shop at a large machine which drilled casings. We worked 12-hour shifts six days a week, six months on nights and six months days.

We had frequent visits from pilots who came to tell us what good work we were doing. We also had prizes for the section that produced the greatest output. A team of us gave up our holiday to work during the Battle of Britain: the RAF was desperate for spares. We each received a Thank You letter from the Managing Director of Hoover's and from the RAF.

By the end of the war I had worked on most of the machines in the factory. It was hard, dirty work, very hot in the summer, with the black-out at night, but I made a lot of friends.

Barbara Hillier worked in a variety of jobs during the war:

In October 1940 I joined the secretarial staff of the Bank of England. We had two months' training on an estate in Gloucestershire, which seemed far removed from the war until we heard the planes going over to bomb Coventry. When we returned to Threadneedle Street we worked two storeys underground in the vault and every so often spent the night in the sub-vault, where they turned off the air-conditioning because it was noisy.

The raids gradually became more sporadic in 1941. By

then I was in a fire-watching team and we slept in shifts, ready to operate the stirrup pumps in the event of incendiary bombs falling on the Bank, but there was never a raid while I was on duty. Tired from bad nights due to air-raids, and tedious, crowded journeys to and from the City, we girls revolted against being treated like school-children and many of us left.

My next job was as secretary to a consulting chemical engineer who was working on war projects. I had a boyfriend who was in the army and stationed at Dover. When he had any leave we went to as many theatres, dances and cinemas as could be crowded in before he returned to the coastal bombardment. I worked in my boss's flat overlooking Kensington Gardens. In the office we had a young Jewish boy who had escaped from Germany and a Jewish girl who had been brought to England by Myra Hess, the pianist, and who never knew what had become of her parents.

At the beginning of 1945 I was called up for war work in a factory making aircraft instruments. To my surprise I was employed as assistant secretary to the Managing Director. There was very little to do except when the regular secretary was absent for a fortnight, having been knocked off her bike in the black-out. Hostilities in Europe ceased while I was working there, but we remained very tense. One day I was having lunch in the factory canteen when someone dropped a tray of crockery; everyone present ducked.

When Betty Bindloss left school she stayed at home in the village of Highweek, Newton Abbot,

Devon, to help her widowed mother, but that did not prevent her from joining in many voluntary activities:

One of the voluntary bodies I joined in the first years of the war, while I was still living at home, was through Guiding. We were called (I think) the "Queen's Messengers" and had a Mobile Feeding Unit, a huge vehicle complete with Soyer boilers and all the equipment necessary for producing food for workers, refugees or evacuated people. Plymouth was the main target in Devon, and on one occasion it was bombed for five nights in succession. After the first night our feeding team of five women set off and stopped in Plymouth's Home Park Football Ground's car park.

We got the Soyer boilers going and for hours fed streams of bombed-out people and exhausted groups of wardens and firemen. When dusk fell we felt sure the bombers would come again so we packed up and trailed slowly out of Plymouth to Harrowbarrow, a village about eight miles off, where we stayed the night, returning to the car park the following morning. This was repeated for three further nights and days. I shall never forget the utter exhaustion of the rescue workers who came for food and sat on the grass and wept with tiredness and the sheer hell of it all.

When bombs were dropped on Newton Abbot station and marshalling yards, the dead and injured were taken to the local hospital and as a Red Cross VAD I was called upon. From then until 1942 I worked at the hospital — in casualty, in the wards and in the theatre. The hospital was short-staffed, and because of that I was given work that would normally have been done by more senior staff.

In 1942 I was called up for full-time nursing. For a frightful six weeks I did absolutely nothing at an isolation hospital near Ivybridge, then I was sent off to Gloucester Hospital, which had become part-civilian, part-services. I was there for 18 months.

Then I was drafted into the RAF, and was a VAD in a huge RAF hospital in Ely. All the wounded airmen who managed to get their bombers back to England from the raids on Germany came to this hospital. I remember especially the burns units and the various treatments that were being tried then. There was a boy of 17 who had wangled his age so that he could get into flying and was burnt literally all over his body. He took two days to die and no painkiller could help at all. His only words during all that time were "Oh Jesus, oh Jesus!"

This was a traumatic two years or so living at top pitch physically and emotionally. After the war I returned home to a completely changed life.

My first need was to take my worn-out mother for a holiday in Cornwall, and then home where she no longer had to make all the decisions or do all the chores. For a time these adjustments took all my thought, energy and capacity. Also I had to come to terms with the loss of so many friends of my own generation

There was a call for women who had already done varied voluntary social work to do a six-month course under the auspices of Josephine Butler. I applied to take the training, was accepted, and began with a couple of months of lectures at Church House, Westminster. Then there were four months of field work with welfare workers in Suffolk; then at a mother and baby home in Penzance; after that in the office in Exeter, working for Exeter Diocese. A committee was formed, and from very small beginnings the Diocesan Adoption Society began work. My part, as the secretary, was to visit applicants from all over Devon, and to write reports on them for the committee to vet before the couples came for an interview. Then, when a suitable match came along, I had to place a baby with them from one of the three or four mother and baby homes in the county and supervise the waiting period in conjunction with the County Council's children's department. In the first year we placed ten babies.

I was paid by the hour and I received initially about 3*s* 6*d* an hour, plus travelling expenses. In those days illegitimacy was still a disgrace and many girls felt that to place their baby for adoption was preferable to involving their parents with an illegitimate grandchild. Every case had a different background, from the promiscuous girl who had been too drunk the night the child was conceived to know who the father was, to the girl and the putative father going through the trauma of parting with their child for its own sake. By the end of ten years we were placing upwards of 50 babies a year.

Elsie Dickinson went to work at 16 after taking her School Certificate:

My father needed a secretary in 1942 when I left Southport High School, so I took over temporarily for £1 1*s* per week, of which I gave my mother £1 for my keep. My father was a plumber and electrician and employed other members of the building trade, which was a reserved occupation. He became an ARP (Air-Raid Precautions) warden and his cousin Norman (his foreman) joined the NFS (National Fire Service). Norman spent nights on end fighting fires at the docks at Bootle and elsewhere near Liverpool. We could see the light of the fires 20 miles away.

After working as secretary, wages clerk (PAYE was introduced while I was there), window dresser and general factotum for four years, I was allowed to take on an assistant. I was in a difficult position — I could not let the family down but had no intention of remaining there for ever. So I trained Margaret to do my job and, after two more years, decided to train to become a teacher. In 1948 as a mature student of 22, I was accepted and able to go to training college. It had been a great effort to tear myself away from the family business, but well worth it.

In 1943 Betty Matson obtained her degree in horticulture:

My first job after graduating was as "gardener" to the research department of Pest Control Ltd at Harston, near Cambridge. I received £190 per annum, out of which I paid about £2 per week for my board and lodging. My work involved growing cereals and weeds in boxes in a greenhouse for the botanists and chemists to spray with weedkiller for research, and breeding locusts for testing insecticides. The locusts required quite a high temperature to survive and breed right through the winter, so electric heaters were installed in greenhouses rented from private owners in the village. It was quite a job keeping the locusts supplied with grass and I got to know the best sources in the local hedgerows and fields. There was an Italian prisoner-of-war camp nearby and some of the prisoners worked for local farmers. On at least one occasion I was followed into a field by a POW who asked: "Have you the time?" I looked at my watch and told him the hour. It was only later that I realised what he was really asking for!

There was no question of having my own flat in those days, so I lodged with a middle-aged couple in a village two and a half miles from my work. My landlady supplemented the food ration by keeping hens in the back garden. Having joined the Red Cross while I was at college, I reported locally and was asked to do occasional night duty at a nearby convalescent home for wounded soldiers. After several months my landlady asked me to find rooms elsewhere. Not until many years later did it occur to me that she may have jumped to the wrong conclusion about my nights out.

The next lodgings I found, with a retired policeman and his wife, were nearer my work, but the conditions were more primitive. They had their own well, and the water had to be pumped up into a tank every morning — 50 strokes of the pump. Friday night was bath night. The bathroom-cum-washhouse opened off the kitchen and the water was heated in a copper, from which it was scooped into the bath. Other days I washed in cold water in the bedroom. On some occasions in the winter I had to break the ice in the jug first and crunch up my flannel, which had frozen solid.

In contrast, when I moved to Surrey in 1945 to run the garden of a private boarding school, I lived in a cottage in the school grounds with a Land Girl, whom I trained. We had water laid on, a gas fire in the sitting-room, a kitchen range (in which we burned wood from the grounds in very cold weather) in the middle room, and a gas stove in the kitchen. We cooked our own breakfast, but had lunch and an evening meal with the school.

The garden and greenhouse had been neglected for some time and, in order to get the ground productive as soon as possible, I used to dig by moonlight. Groups of pupils were sent out from time to time to help "Dig for Victory". As soon as some vegetables were available, they were taken up to the school kitchen.

Margaret McDonald has always been ready to accept a challenge:

By January 1940 I had been in the ATS for four months. The platoon was already full when I was called up in September 1939, except for two vacancies for cooks. I said I could not cook, but the commanding officer assured me I would be taught. This did not happen, but I found myself being expected to cook for 42 officers. Fortunately I was still living at home, and I was able to ask for the menu for the following day, then go home and ask my mother how to cook the food. This worked very successfully except on a couple of occasions when the sergeant-major — a

111

terrifying battle-axe — changed the menu. However, I was very lucky: I only made sago pudding in mistake for rice and produced a highly original fish pie which the mess orderlies were very reluctant to serve, but they were confounded when the officers asked for second helpings!

By January 1940, however, I was working at Church Crookham for the Royal Army Medical Corps as part of a team cooking for a thousand men. This was soul-destroying and very hard work — for example beating up 100 lb flour to make a Yorkshire pudding!

The Army, in its bureaucratic manner, required all kinds of weekly returns, one of them being an account of the platoon's level of education. I was the only one with both Matriculation and Higher Schools, so I was transferred as a clerk and was soon a sergeant.

Army life, in spite of a war, was a very happy and fulfilling experience and I missed the wonderful comradeship when the war ended.

Teaching in wartime conditions posed various problems for Iris Harris:

Because young male teachers had joined the Forces, there was no difficulty in getting a teaching job when I left college in 1942. I went to an infants' school in East Barnet, which had been forced to share a building with a secondary school, as theirs had been commandeered by the Fire Service. We were not made to feel very welcome: we were not allowed into their staff-room and we were put on the top floor, so that going to the basement during air-raids took longer than teachers with the older children.

I had been taught that each child should develop individually so I was dismayed when I was confronted with 55 five-year-olds and very few stationery supplies. I had to adapt very quickly to a workable way of teaching.

Once I was in the basement shelters with my 55 little ones for many hours because (although we did not know it at the time) the V1s were appearing over London. I got into dreadful trouble because I spilled red ink over what was then the sacrosanct register. No biros in those days!

I married in April 1945 when the buzz bombs or doodlebugs were still coming, and I remember thinking, "Just let me get married before I'm hit by one!"

Options were limited for anyone having to choose a career during the war, and Ian Sandeman therefore decided on the Royal Navy:

From the age of 15 I had to think seriously about my future career. At King's School, Bruton, we would have been expected in peacetime to go on to university, but in wartime with every male liable to be called up from the age of 18, our horizon was limited to the Armed Forces, or some other form of National Service. I decided to follow my brother into the Royal Navy, a choice dictated by the fact that one could live reasonably comfortably in a ship (provided it did not sink), whereas a soldier had to carry all his belongings around with him, often in very mucky conditions, and the only aspect of the Royal Air Force that appealed to a teenager — flying — seemed a most hazardous activity in wartime. I harboured no heroic ambitions.

113

I accordingly opted to work for the exam for entry to the Royal Navy as an officer cadet and, as a second choice, I applied for officer entry to the Royal Naval Volunteer Reserve. My main memory from then on was struggling to raise my mathematical prowess to the level required to pass the exam, assisted and encouraged by an elderly teacher, who plied me incessantly with past exam papers. I sat the exam early in 1945 and, much to my — and everyone's — amazement, passed on the first occasion. My success was due mainly to my marks in French. I only just scraped through in maths.

I was appointed Cadet, Royal Navy, on 1 May 1945, and two days after VE Day I joined the Royal Naval College. At that time the college was accommodated at Eaton Hall, the property of the Duke of Westminster, near Chester, having been evacuated from Dartmouth when the buildings suffered some bomb damage. They were later used by the American Forces in their preparations for D-Day.

About 90 cadets assembled at Eaton Hall for our basic naval training. We were known as "Special Entry" cadets, i.e. public school entry, as distinct from the 300 or so "Dart" cadets, who at that time used to begin their naval life at the age of 14. Nissen huts in the grounds of the Hall were used as sleeping accommodation and classrooms, and we fed at separate tables in the main dining hut, which served all the cadets in the college. The ration scales were much more lavish than those for civilians.

The main building of the Hall itself accommodated the officers on the staff of the college and some classrooms used by the "Darts", so we rarely had occasion to cross the "sacred" threshold. The River Dee ran through the grounds of the Hall and was used for boatwork training, the part of the syllabus I found most enjoyable.

We spent the summer at Eaton Hall, after which we were allowed to progress to the Cadet Training Cruiser, HMS *Frobisher*, a 27-year-old vessel which had been hurriedly reconverted from her war status after VE Day. Including our "Dart" contemporaries, we totalled about 180 cadets, and formed the bulk of the ship's complement, being employed on every kind of menial task in the various departments of the ship.

We spent eight months in *Frobisher*. Life on board was rigorous compared to that at the Naval College. We lived in "broadside messes", not unlike those of Nelson's day, except that there were no guns in the mess space, a large area in which we ate, slept and spent our off-duty periods. The main pipe carrying superheated steam from the boiler-rooms to the engine-room was immediately beneath this space, which was pleasant enough in the English winter, but it was almost unbearable in hot weather. We slept in hammocks above the mess tables or in odd corners of the ship, and were brutally awakened at a very early hour each morning by a bugle call. We had 20 minutes in which to get dressed, lash up and stow away our hammocks and muster for duty on the quarterdeck.

Our first task of the day, before breakfast, was always to scrub the wooden decks with long-handled scrubbers and salt water — and always in bare feet. This was quite pleasant in West Indian waters, but when there was ice and snow on deck it was a different matter. Our routine included classroom training in various naval subjects, and we also received much practical instruction, for example, we were required to assist in the navigation of the ship when at sea.

On passing my basic training examinations I was promoted to the rank of midshipman and appointed in May 1946 to HMS *King George V*, one of our largest battleships and also the flagship of the Commander-in-Chief, Home Fleet. The year 1946 was one of national retrenchment and recovery from the war and, while the Home Fleet was still in being, it was rapidly losing many of its ships as they were paid off into reserve. So the C-in-C had little to command, and during my few months in the flagship we rarely worked in company with other ships.

Later that year I was appointed to the cruiser HMS *Sheffield*, flagship of the America and West Indies Squadron, based in Bermuda. There were six ships in the squadron, which was responsible for providing a Royal Naval "presence" around the whole of North and South America, and among the various offshore island colonies. The high spot of my eight months in the ship was a three-month circuit of South America, "showing the flag" in a dozen ports. We were the first British warship to visit South America since the war, and so the programme of four or five days in each port, followed by only one or two nights at sea before the next round of social activities, was exhausting.

CHAPTER
FIVE

Transport and Holidays

The Government had taken over the four main railway companies and the London Passenger Transport Board on 1 September 1939. In June 1940 names were removed from all but the smallest stations and this, added to the black-out, made travelling by train a nightmare. At first all the internal lighting was removed, but later some light was possible, with blinds pulled down.

Pressure on the railways was tremendous, as they were used to convey thousands of troops to their destinations, especially at such times as Dunkirk and D-Day. In addition to special trains for the Forces, railways had to transport food, shells, fuel and other necessities, so there was little room for ordinary passengers. "Is your journey really necessary?" was a reminder to civilians of the importance of rail transport; in fact travelling was so uncomfortable that no one was likely to use the train unnecessarily. People, many of them standing, were crammed into the coaches and corridors of long-distance trains, along with all their luggage. Toilets were usually occupied by as many people as could cram themselves in, and to use them for their normal purpose was difficult. To clamber over the sleeping bodies in the corridor was only the first obstacle. Those who managed to sleep on the luggage rack were the fortunate ones.

Journeys at night, once the names of stations had been removed, was unnerving. Even those who knew the route well were confused, and if you were making the journey for the first time it was impossible to know where you were, unless some other passenger recognised the station and could help. At least if you were going to the terminus you knew when you had arrived. At first when there was a raid the train stopped at the next station, so that anyone who wished could alight; then the train was allowed to proceed at only 15 miles an hour, incurring long delays. This rule was abolished in February 1941 except at night, when the speed was reduced to 30 miles an hour during an alert.

There were very few restaurant cars and by 1942 they were provided in only 72 trains; even these were removed in April 1944. One day Freddie Grisewood had to stand all the way from London to Sunderland when he was going to speak to a large audience on behalf of the Kitchen Front. There were no refreshments, then after a bun and cup of tea he had to stand all the way home again. This was quite a common experience.

The London Underground was considered one of the safest places during raids, the chief danger being that of flooding. Flood gates were installed but no trains ran under the Thames during a raid, so passengers risked being turned out at the Strand or Waterloo during an alert. Other stations at risk were closed, but trains continued to run through them without stopping. The deeper stations were soon used as air-raid shelters, with special bunks installed and facilities provided.

Petrol rationing was introduced within the first weeks of the war. Every owner was allowed a basic ration according to the size of the car, with supplementary petrol coupons issued for essential business or domestic purposes. Some turned to producer-gas, towing a burner and converter behind the vehicle, but they needed a lot of maintenance and finally shortage of solid fuel made them unviable. As petrol became more scarce, with the needs of the Forces predominant, the basic ration was reduced and then finally cancelled altogether on 13 March 1942. Petrol was granted only if proved absolutely essential. Laying the cars up for the duration was a complicated business and some people had difficulty restarting them when the war ended.

Doctors were among the few civilians who were allowed petrol, but they had difficulty in getting their cars serviced. Farmers, too, had a ration for essential work.

Shortage of supplies meant a severe cut in oil and petrol to London Transport buses, which, added to the call-up of many personnel, led to a severe cut in services, just at a time when former car users were having to rely on them. In April 1942 orderly queuing became compulsory, avoiding the former free-for-all. So many buses were damaged during the first few weeks of the blitz that London Transport had to appeal for other bus companies to lend them theirs, and many responded. Drivers found the black-out a great strain on their eyes.

During the war few people were able to go on holiday, and probably felt guilty if they did. Many used the break to help on a farm, pick fruit or go "hopping". Others on vital work often gave up their holidays to help with the war effort. After VE Day things slowly began to change. Husbands and boyfriends were eventually discharged from the Forces; gradually more cars appeared on the roads and public transport improved, so it was possible to enjoy short outings. Hotels that had been commandeered were returned to private use; others that had been bombed were restored; and gradually beaches that had been mined and protected with barbed wire were cleared.

With no petrol available for private cars, Betty Matson was glad of her bicycle during the war:

The first bicycle I possessed I bought in 1940 in my first year at college, from a fellow student for five shillings (25p). This enabled me to cycle into Nottingham or Loughborough for shopping, and to go with a friend on

Youth Hostelling tours to the Peak District at half-term. One afternoon we could not make the hostel before dark (no advance booking was necessary then) and stopped at a café where the dear lady gave us cocoa and sandwiches, comfortable beds, and a full English breakfast. When we enquired what we owed her she said her usual charge was five shillings, but as we were students she would charge only two and six.

While at college we found that hitch-hiking was a cheap and interesting way to travel (though the Principal tried to stop it). Two friends once spent their journey comfortably on a sofa in the back of a furniture van. Another pair hitched a covered lorry and sat in the cabin with the driver. When they asked what was in the back he said he would tell them when they got off. When they reached their destination they asked him again and he said: "Bombs!"

Almost all cars had to be demobilised and the rotor cap from the engine deposited at the Council offices. My father had to cycle to work, approximately three miles, the first part up a long hill. I believe he was able to manage this without getting off and walking, as he had three-speed gears. In the mid- and late Forties I occasionally managed this myself, with no gears, if there was a strong following wind, or by zigzagging from side to side of the road. There was very little motor traffic!

My first job was in Harston, near Cambridge. I had lodgings in Trumpington and cycled to work every day — two and a half miles each way, and back for lunch. Whether I was going to or from work, the wind always seemed to be against me.

I was able to travel home by train for occasional

weekends, Cambridge to King's Cross then Fenchurch Street to Benfleet, Essex. In the summer of 1944, when the doodlebugs started, my mother sent a telegram telling me not to go home because of the risk of the bombs falling on London. I thought, "If I can't go by train, I'll cycle." I worked on Saturday morning, but set off after a quick lunch and got home in good time for supper. It was approximately 60 miles and I did the journey in almost exactly six and a half hours, with a half-hour break about half-way. Once or twice I stopped for a glass of lemonade at a pub — very daring in those days! On one occasion I remember joining my sister for a game of tennis on the Saturday evening and going for a swim off Canvey Island on the Sunday morning, leaving home at 4.30 p.m. and getting back to Trumpington at 11 p.m., when it was still light (double Summer Time).

I reckoned that this old bike carried me for at least 2000 miles before I got another, a second-hand Hercules, for £5.

Grace Horseman describes the difficulty of getting across London during the blitz:

Originally, May & Baker's factory and offices, where I worked, had been in Wandsworth, where I lived, so when the business moved to Dagenham, arrangements were made for a lorry to transport workers there daily. It left around 6 a.m., rather early for me, but later I was able to get a lift home at night if I was ready in time. We passed through the East End of London and the dock area, so saw the devastation wrought by the bombs, with fires still burning. Sometimes when the sirens sounded we saw a pathetic procession of people, many of them Jews, with their bundles of bedding, making for the nearest underground shelter.

The Germans loved rainy days, when there was plenty of cover from our fighters. One dismal wet day, after many alerts, I was at last on my way home on the District Line from Dagenham. We had not gone far when we stopped, and waited, and waited. At last we began moving again, but only for a few yards, when we stopped again, and waited, and waited. It was stop and start, stop and start, for over an hour, and this was only the beginning of my journey, with many bombs exploding around us. Later we learnt that a barrage balloon had broken loose and was trailing along the railway track. I was worried about getting home, so someone suggested it would be a good idea to transfer to the Northern Line. This meant walking across London Bridge in the dark. No one else was about, and there was the incessant sound of explosions from bombs and anti-aircraft guns, with flashes of light revealing the empty bridge. I have never felt so vulnerable, and it was with relief that I finally reached London Bridge Station.

However, that was not the end of my problems. During raids certain underground stations that were vulnerable to flooding were closed until the All Clear, and Tooting Broadway, where I was aiming, was one of them. So I had to go on to Colliers Wood, an unknown destination as far as I was concerned. Fortunately a gentleman also wanted Tooting Broadway and offered to accompany me. So at least I had company as I walked through the bomb-ridden streets. Then at Tooting Broadway I was delighted to find a tram that was going to Wandsworth, and gladly found a seat. Not for long! Soon the tram was stopped just before we reached Waldron Road School, which was ablaze, with fire-fighters and their hoses in all directions. We all had to alight. Once there was a good fire, the German bombers used it to direct their loads, and there were plenty of them about. Again I began walking. I eventually reached home after 9 p.m. When Mother opened the door she burst into tears. She and my father felt sure I must have been a casualty.

Once the war had ended it was much easier to get away for holidays, and Nina Armour made good use of the opportunities:

During the summer term at the Central School, there were notices on the board inviting students to try farm camp holidays. Free accommodation, food and a little pay were offered in exchange for work in the fresh air on farms. Three of us at the art school had tried this in 1945, when we went to a farm camp near Twyford, in Berkshire. There we met factory workers, shop assistants and teachers, among others. Many people liked the idea of spending a holiday in this way, and it was stimulating meeting so many different people. We sang while travelling to farms in lorries, and in the evenings we walked to the village pub or joined a local dance. We returned to London with a great feeling of well-being.

So in 1946 we decided to do it again, this time travelling further afield, to Cornwall. It took at least eight hours to reach Penzance, where we were met and taken to a converted manor house not far away. It had been used by the Land Army during the war. We slept in bunks, in a large room, and ate in a dining hall. Round the house was a charming but delapidated garden, with a distant view of the sea and St Michael's Mount.

We planted anemone corms, which looked like bits of dried earth and were difficult to find if dropped in the wrong place. We also helped with the harvest, as I was reminded when I found an old photograph taken at the time, with two of us and the farmer on a cart with a horse in front.

After the Cornish holiday, I was to travel to the south of France, to have a holiday with Mother, who was travelling there from Berlin. We were to meet in Paris. My friend Phil, also from the Central School, was to travel with me, which made it much more fun. Before we went, Phil's mother came up to the flat unexpectedly to have a look at me, as we had not met before. It just so happened that I was turning out the flat and giving it a good clean and polish, which really impressed Phil's mother. After that she was quite happy for her daughter to travel with me!

Phil and I travelled from Victoria to Dover, crossed by boat to Calais and then went to Paris by train. We had hoped to meet my mother at the Gare du Nord, where we first arrived. As there was no sign of her we went on as planned, by Metro, to the Gare de Lyon, where we were to catch our train for Cannes. Still no sign of Mother. However, we were able to find seats on the train and hoped for the best. It was not until the train had been going for some time that my mother suddenly appeared. We reached

125

Cannes after a cramped night in the railway carriage, existing on sandwiches and fruit.

In the summer of 1947 I went to Berlin to stay with Mother. I had finished at the Central School by then and I stayed away the whole summer.

Although I had travelled a great deal before the war as a child, I had never travelled alone and it was quite an adventure. I bought myself a suit in dark brown, fine material with a pinstripe. Clothes were still on coupons, and it was best to buy good quality if one could. One could go anywhere in a suit and feel comfortable. I bought a little brown hat to match, and with brown accessories I had already, the whole outfit was quite smart and it gave me confidence. I also bought a large suitcase.

My mother and Michael Lessin, my stepfather-to-be, were at the station in Berlin to meet me, and I gradually became acquainted with post-war Berlin and the lives of some members of the Control Commission, where Mother worked.

By this time my mother had been in Berlin nearly two years. She looked very well and much younger than when she had left England in 1945. She had had a hard war and the wear and tear had left their mark. Now, with no household chores and responsibilities, the cheerful company of many pleasant people revived her former sparkle. She worked hard, as did many of the people out there, but was able to enjoy to the full her leisure time. She would go walking in the Grünewald, and horseriding. Sometimes she went swimming or spent time being sociable at one of the many clubs. The Gatow Country Club, on the edge of one of the large Berlin lakes, had been a great favourite with the Nazi officials and was now enjoyed by the British. There were many receptions in the evenings.

Mother and Michael Lessin wanted to get married in England and we all travelled back together for the event.

I began working for Bakelite Ltd, and often at weekends went walking in the country with a group. One of the group leaders was to lead a two-week holiday to Switzerland and I decided to join them. We were staying at Finhaut, a very small resort reached by a mountain railway that went through to Chamonix. There was no road at that time, and no cars polluted the atmosphere. The air was quite unlike any I had breathed before and made me feel full of energy. The water tasted wonderful, and everything was incredibly clean and sparkling. Coming out of tired, post-war England, it was a joy to wander into the little shops and handle the colourful pretty woollen jumpers and cardigans, socks, gloves and scarves, and buy what we wanted. The exchange rate then was good for us, and things were not expensive.

On this holiday I met Charles Armour. A year later, in July 1949, we were married and came again to Switzerland for our honeymoon.

Travelling in India was an exciting adventure, and Elsie Paget much enjoyed her visit to Benares:

Early in 1940, while my husband Leslie and I were wondering about the new war radios which were used for the benefit of all (including the whole street), we had a

127

short holiday from Raniganj for two days to visit Benares. Leslie had made arrangements to see a clergyman there.

Railway travel catered for everyone. First Class was generally for VIPs — Government officials, Senior Army officers, Indian royalty, heads of companies and so on. Second Class was for all well-to-do people, even occasionally missionaries with families on a longish journey, but we usually travelled Inter (meaning between Second and Third). This was for all castes, including outcasts. In my early days, especially while working for the first Bengali exam, Third was very helpful. No one could speak English but everyone was anxious to help this odd white woman to understand and speak Bengali. Passengers felt that if one of these Europeans *chose* to travel Third, she must have fellow-feeling.

On one occasion a mother getting two or three children into the train plonked her rather dirty but very sweet baby on my knees (a convenient place where she reckoned it would be held and not allowed to roll off). The baby did not seem to mind and neither did I. Little children respond quickly to strangers their parents appear to approve. Sometimes a little hand would gently touch my arm or hand, I suppose to see if the white would come off.

On one journey the train had to stop at a small station as we had a "hot axle" — a frequent happening in the hot season. Being still, it felt hotter than ever. A little boy, feeling particularly hot, cried and cried and, seeing the train was standing still, yelled all the more. His mother did a wise thing. We were allowed to get off the train as long as some railway official approved. She took the little fellow to a stand-pipe tap, and filled two buckets with water. The little boy stopped his yelling and stood still, ready for anything mother might choose to do. She emptied the first bucket in one glad splash all over him. Chuckles and shouts of joy! Then she took the second bucketful and, slowly, making the most of every drop, poured it over him in small quantities. Result — bliss! Back into the train. Wet clothes? That little mattered; it was so hot that clothes dried very quickly, and the process was enjoyably cool.

When we went to Benares we decided to leave Raniganj early on the morning of the first day, and return fairly late on the second day. We lived less than a quarter of a mile from the station, which was very much closer than in most towns and villages, which were scattered over the wide area of East Bengal. Some years later we lived where we had a bus ride of 23 miles to the railway station, and later still at a more remote part where we could travel to the station only by bullock cart, as there was no proper road. Someone has described these trips as "monotonously beautiful and unceasingly interesting" — trees of so many varieties, shrubs, ponds, streams, lotus flowers, waterlilies, birds, and small wild animals.

The Holy City of Benares is holy perhaps because of the Holy River of the Ganges, on which Benares is built. The clergyman friend who had invited us said he would meet us at the station, take us home and have tiffin (a short early lunch), after which matters connected with the church could be discussed, not least the ever-present Hindu-Muslim animosity. Leslie told of an experience we had had in Raniganj that had kept the people giggling for several days, a welcome matter to cheer an atmosphere that could become "explosive" with Hindus and Muslims at times.

CHAPTER
SIX

Sport and Recreation

On the declaration of war all forms of entertainment, including football, greyhound and racing fixtures, were cancelled. There was public uproar and the Government soon recognised their mistake and withdrew the restriction by the end of October 1939. However, the absence of professional and amateur players meant much less sport was played during the war.

Schools also suffered, with sports fields being used sometimes for air-raid shelters or allotments. Air-raids also cut down the time available for sports: exposure could be dangerous if a lone plane straffed the area.

Golf courses and sports grounds made excellent landing fields for enemy aircraft, so when an invasion became more and more likely in 1940 it was important that they should be immobilised by planting obstructions on them. People were asked to help dig up golf courses. Food was grown on some playing fields, or they were used for drill for the Home Guard and other purposes.

When the war was over Football League matches were resumed, Liverpool becoming champions in 1946-7, Arsenal in 1947-8, and Portsmouth the following two years. In 1947 Denis Compton, the cricketer, was nominated the Sportsman of the Year by the *Daily Express.*

In 1948 the Olympic Games were held in Britain for the first time for 40 years. Britain managed to win just four silver medals against America's twelve golds. Fanny Blankers-Koen of Holland was one of the greatest female athletes of the century and won four gold medals.

Although television was introduced in 1936 it was shut down during the war. At first only homes within 30 miles radius of London could receive programmes and then only for two short periods daily, but by 1949 TV had also spread to the Midlands. It was wireless that was the lifeline for news and entertainment during the war. People wanted to escape from the harsh realities of war, so comedies such as *ITMA* (*It's That Man Again*), starring Tommy Handley, were popular.

Cinema programmes finished by 11p.m. Moreover, to accommodate soldiers and workers away from home, many cinemas opened on Sundays, but often showing inferior films. Once air-raids began, managers had to announce the alert so that those who wished could leave the cinema, but this became such a frequent occurrence that instead they flashed a message on the screen announcing, "An air-raid warning has just been sounded. If you wish to leave the cinema, please do so as quietly as possible. Those who wish to remain may do so at their own risk. The film now continues." This would be followed eventually by the All Clear notice. Although in the early days many left, it was not long before everyone stayed to see the film through. As well as the normal pattern of a main feature, a supporting film and newsreel, the Ministry of Information added a propaganda film, so programmes became longer and longer. With no television, newsreels were particularly popular.

The British film industry flourished under war conditions. The documentary *Target for Tonight* in 1941, about a raid on Germany by Wellington F for Freddie, with real airmen as actors, provided a breakthrough. *Coastal Command* was even better, and in March 1943 *Desert Victory* showed the Army in action, whilst *Western Approaches*, released in 1943, told the story of merchant seamen on Atlantic convoys.

There were also many excellent non-war films, including *Kipps*, *Major Barbara*, *Dear Octopus* and Noël Coward's *Blithe Spirit.* Towards the end of the decade the British company Ealing Studios produced some famous comedies, among them *Whisky Galore* and *Passport to Pimlico.* The theatre was equally popular, with queues forming early, in spite of the threat of raids. The musical *Oklahoma* opened in New York in 1943 but was soon to be enjoyed in the UK. Christopher Fry's play *The Lady's Not for Burning* was first performed in 1949.

Promenade Concerts were very popular but music was affected by the wartime atmosphere as much as films and theatre. Non-classical music continued to be in demand, and many bands became famous. In the early Forties the saxophonist Charlie Parker helped introduce a new form of jazz called bebop. Dance halls were full throughout the war, and the Lyceum in London was invariably crowded with servicemen and girls meeting regularly and dancing to live music. Most local dances had to make do with records.

The BBC appreciated the importance of combating boredom among factory workers, so in June 1940 they introduced two special half-hour programmes at 10.30 a.m. and 3.30 p.m. This break was soon known as "Music While You Work" and was so popular it continued long after the war. Vocal programmes could be disruptive as workers tried to take down the words, so many famous bands broadcast orchestral music.

ENSA (Entertainments National Services Association) was already providing entertainment for the troops, and in July 1940 they gave their first dinner-hour performance to factory workers at Woolwich Arsenal. Many more performances followed. Conditions were not ideal amid the clatter of cutlery, and often players were exhausted, having endured very difficult journeys on overcrowded trains, but their efforts were appreciated.

Many of the classics were reread during the war, often by candlelight in shelters. Dickens, Jane

Austen and others seemed to give a sense of normality; John Galsworthy's *Forsyte Saga* and Tolstoy's *War and Peace* were also read. Current writers included Ernest Hemingway with his classic *For Whom the Bell Tolls* (1940), Monica Dickens and A. J. Cronin. *The Four Quartets*, T. S. Eliot's poem published in 1944, includes a description of London during the blitz. He received the Nobel Prize in 1948. George Orwell's novel *Animal Farm* a satire on Communism, was published in 1945.

Dr Benjamin Spock's influential *Common Sense Book of Baby and Child Care*, published in 1946, liberated babies' lives from rigid routines. In quite a different way Anne Frank's diary, published in 1947, had a profound effect on all those who read it. She was a Jew, only 13 years old in 1942 when she was given the diary. She kept it until 4 August 1944, when the family's hiding place was discovered and they were taken to concentration camps. Anne and her sister died of typhus there in March 1945. Fortunately the diary was found and kept safe by Dutch friends.

Shortage of paper not only curtailed the printing of books but also meant that newspapers were drastically reduced in size, and as fewer copies were printed, they were often in short supply.

Alongside his academic achievements at Glasgow University, Graham Jardine much enjoyed taking part in competitive athletics, achieving some distinction:

My recreational obsessions — athletics and cross-country running — began early in the summer of 1940, when I was still at school. Athletics continued to provide exercise and pleasure at Glasgow University and in the wider world of open sports meetings in spring and summer from 1945 to 1949, despite my having to accept that hurdling was no longer *my* event; the hurdles were now 3 ft 6 in. in height and I was little more than two feet taller! Now, however, there were 880-yard and one-mile races to compete in, and since these seemed to suit my stamina, I began participating in them — although their pace was still a bit too fast and their distances too short for my performances to be very successful.

All the intra- and inter-university races were scratch events; all the competitors started together. This is the case at present in most events, whether restricted or open, now that athletics has become a sport that is highly marketable on television and, indeed, in packed indoor and outdoor stadiums. In the Forties the vast majority of athletes were true amateurs; they participated for the love of the exercise and the thrill of the competition, and there were no prearranged pacemakers in either championship or show-piece events, as there often are now. On the other hand, and thankfully, there were many sports meetings, both large and small, in which the keen though mediocre athlete could compete against star performers and have a fair chance of winning a first, second or third prize. This was possible because of the system of handicapping. For example, in a 100-yard race, up to 11 or 12 yards might be "given away" by the back-marker and in an 880-yard race the front-marker might be starting 50 or 60 yards short of the full distance. In Scotland, certainly, handicaps were very strictly controlled by a National Handicapper, who based a person's handicap, in any particular race, on performances — especially prize-winning placings — in recent races.

There was also an enormous difference between the tracks of those days and the *tartan* tracks that are so common now. At most sports meetings — even at the famous Rangers' Sports that took place annually at Ibrox Stadium, Glasgow, on the first Saturday in August — the 100-yard races were run on grass. Many of the tracks at local sports meetings were also marked out on grass. It was only at the bigger meetings, such as the Glasgow Police Sports, which took place at Hampden Stadium, and at the Rangers' Sports, that there were "cinder" tracks.

Much though I enjoyed taking part in athletics while a schoolboy and a university student, the real recreational benefit of arrival at university in the mid-Forties was the opportunity to take part in cross-country running. Cross-country runners at Glasgow University are members of the Hares and Hounds Section of Glasgow University Athletic Club, and the Section began its life in October 1921. Saturday, 14 October 1944, however, was the day of *my* first run. We covered a distance of about five and a half miles, which was five miles farther than I had ever run before. The course included tarmac-surfaced roads, the towpath of the Forth and Clyde Canal, grass-covered fields, a road with a steep uphill gradient that went on for about 350 yards, and several heavily ploughed fields. One of the runners, who at one point chose to take a short cut, found himself stuck in a marsh — in his glossy dancing shoes, for in those wartime days sandshoes (plimsolls) were difficult to obtain and he therefore wore the lightest footwear he possessed.

A few weeks later I was beginning to dream of running for Glasgow against Aberdeen, Edinburgh and St Andrew's universities in the home or away matches that were to take place between November 1944 and February 1945. However, I was not old enough to be permitted to compete in such long races. My chance came on 24 March 1945, less than two weeks after my 18th birthday, when, with seven other Glasgow runners, I travelled to Aberdeen for the first time and took part in the Scottish Universities' Cross-Country Championship race. Glasgow had won this race in 1944, but in the 1944-5 season had lost matches, twice to Edinburgh and once to St Andrew's. My delight at being one of the "counting six" of the Glasgow team that won that day can well be imagined. On the evening after the race there was a dance in the Students' Union — which at that time was the only "mixed" university union, certainly in Scotland. Around midnight, the Glasgow team, led by a prominent member of the Aberdeen team, sang their way happily through the deserted streets of the city to their spartan overnight accommodation. In the black-out the master-switch of the building could not be found. Perhaps this was just as well, for, as we discovered in the morning, the camp-beds we had passed the night on were stretchers — and we were housed in a First Aid hut at a location that hindsight suggests was in the vicinity of Foresterhill Hospital.

The Hares and Hounds' Captain, Secretary and Treasurer of the 1944-5 season had all been final-year medical students. As a result, at the AGM of the section in March 1945 their positions were taken over by other members of the victorious Glasgow team. I thus found myself launched, first as Treasurer, into a lifetime of administrative responsibilities — in a multitude of local, national and international organisations — that have sometimes provided a challenge and have always given a great deal of satisfaction.

With the end of hostilities the traditional match between Glasgow University and Trinity College, Dublin, was revived on 15 December 1945, and Dublin was the venue. The Glasgow team left home on Thursday the 13th, slept overnight on the boat in harbour, sailed on the 14th from Stranraer to Larne, and thence travelled by train to Belfast and, eventually, to Dublin (en route the boiler of the train's engine blew up, causing a minor derailment and a two-hour delay). On our arrival, most of us were accommodated in rooms in Trinity College but our Secretary was put up in the home of Trinity's Secretary. At the end of the weekend, spent in a city that had no rationing, all of us except our Secretary sailed from Larne to Stranraer, some of us in possession of silk stockings destined to bring delight to sisters and sweethearts, and all of us impecunious except, quite literally, for one silver sixpence amongst us. Our Secretary, meantime, was still in Dublin, for he had taken a fancy to one of the sisters of the Trinity Secretary.

A few weeks later, when the new university term started, he had not yet returned to Glasgow. The rumour, of course, was that he was still in Dublin but, in truth, he had received his call-up papers to the Army over the Christmas holidays. As a result, I took over the secretarial duties from January until October 1946, when it was the Captain's shoes that I had to fill, since he, in turn, had gone off to serve His Majesty. (My turn came later, from 1950 to 1952 when first the King and then the Queen required me.)

Gary Cornford had cousins living nearby who could share adventures with him and his sister, Rosemary:

As little children we spent much of our time with our cousins, on the lawn at Granny Crouch's cottage in the village, playing at Chestnut Cottages, or going on long walks. Mum pushed Rosemary and me in a huge black pram. Aunty Dorothy and Aunty Ethel must have had some form of transport for Peter and Alan but I can only remember our pram, often with all four of us kids in it. We would be accompanied by Granny Crouch.

Our walks were sometimes to Cowbeech and back to see Aunty Lil and Uncle Stan. (Their children Peg and Stanley were grown up. Peg was in the Women's Land Army and Stanley in the Army as an engineer.) The other route was a triangular trip round "the mountain", with a stop to slide down the steep banks by the rectory and look at the initials carved on the trunks of the old beech trees.

Dad was marshlands officer for the Ministry of Agriculture. We were lucky to have our dad around during the war, but his days were long and we saw little of him.

139

His job required the use of a car and he had a Standard 10. We were thus able to go out for trips if the petrol ration allowed.

The favourite pastime for the cousins (me, Pete, Alan and Rosemary tagging along) was either "coalmining" or "making sand". Being wartime, the toys we had were dolls made by mum, the aunts or our big cousins. However, the gardens and fields of Chestnut Cottages were our playroom.

"Coalmining" consisted of digging a hole about three feet deep and three feet in diameter. We could not get beyond three feet because of heavy clay. Once dug, the "coalmine" manifested itself as a cave, a wartime trench, a dungeon or whatever. Mum would bring out drinks and snacks, which we ate crouched in the hole. Finally, when we had squeezed the last drop of fun from our coalmine, we filled it in again. In time the need to dig came on us again and a new hole would be dug.

Then one fateful day in 1942 we dug the last coalmine. Mum had just given birth to Barbara, and Aunty Ethel was looking after us. At this time I had my first bicycle — a fairy cycle. We all learnt to ride at an early age. Like most kids, I always "forgot" to put my bike away in the shed at the bottom of the garden.

So, on a lovely warm spring morning the cousins set to work to dig the biggest coalmine yet. As usual we played our games in it and had our snacks. As the day wore on we began to lose interest. Mum was in bed with the baby. Normally she would come up with some brilliant idea to raise our flagging spirits. As boredom got the better of us, I had an idea. "Let's make a pond!" Being the eldest and on home territory gave me some authority. So we filled buckets and emptied them into the hole. Having done so we realised there wasn't much we could do with it so, wet and muddy, we left it. Thanks to the clay layer the water did not drain away and that night, when dad returned from work, he didn't notice the "pond" as he took my fairy cycle to the shed — at least, he didn't notice it until he fell in.

The next day, as the cousins gathered, my dad ordered us to fill in the hole. My 18-stone father, when angry, would have repelled the German army. We shovelled as though our lives depended upon it. The water and clay now formed a slippery sea of mud. In my panic, I lost my balance and fell in. Imagine my humiliation when Aunty Ethel couldn't find me any clean pants and I had to wear a pair of Rosemary's knickers! Thus our careers as coalminers came to an early and, in my case, sticky end.

"Making sand" consisted of sitting on the concrete path and using hammers to pound bits of brick, coal and rock into powder. This was seived through tea-strainers and put into narrow jars in coloured layers. We had not heard of Alum Bay at that time. Of course, it may have been my mother's idea. She was incredibly inventive and encouraged us in all kinds of activities. Her reward was to see her lovely sandstone rockery in the front garden reduced to fine sand through the long years of the war. I doubt that many parents would have allowed such "vandalism". However, my mum's generosity and encouragement were equal to the best teacher's and we grew up to be artistic, inventive and precocious readers, and devoted to our mum. We would all sit on the carpet in front

141

of the fire while Mum read the comic strips from the *Daily Mirror*. Every day we followed the adventure of Garth, Ruggles, Jane and Pip, Squeak and Wilfred. In later years we had our own weekly comics, including *Eagle*, *Girls' Own* and *Bunty*. My sister probably had *Sunny Stories* as well.

French studies for Gill Meason included recreational activities:

On one occasion the whole school went across the road to the cinema to see the wonderful film of *Henry V* with Laurence Olivier. It was a thrill to go to the cinema for a Technicolor film, instead of seeing old black-and-white films from the school projector in the hall.

Another time the French film *La Kermesse Héroïque* was shown at Ware cinema. Half the school took the train to Ware and walked back, the other half walked there and took the train back. The film was boring and the sound track so bad that the educational value was nil; however, there were boys from a local school to provide excitement! Further amusement was caused because, in deference to our Allies, a record of "La Marseillaise" had been acquired. Unfortunately it was a version intended to accompany the singing of the whole anthem. After each verse we sat down only to leap up as the orchestra struck up again.

In 1946 I went to France for the first time. I was studying French and German for Higher School Certificate, and my French teacher was able to arrange an exchange for me.

The weekend that I arrived, there was a fête in the small town where I was staying. I was pressured into entering a talent contest by singing "It's a long way to Tipperary". The winner was decided by the amount of applause and I was overwhelmed by the warmth of my reception, putting me in second place after a popular, buxom, local lady who sang "La Vie en Rose".

I loved staying with my host family. Every morning I sat in the sunny yard with 14-year-old Hélène, peeling the vegetables for the daily soup, while she taught me French folk songs. In the afternoon we often visited Hélène's friends to play games, drink tea and, to my amazement, smoke under the watchful eye of the mothers. I declined!

Isla Brownless remembers some concerts at school:

Concerts were special occasions, oases of sanity and calm in an upside-down world. Twice a term some international musician came to play in Big School at Wycombe Abbey. The town came as well to hear Jelly d'Aranyi, Dame Myra Hess, Heddle Nash, Solomon, and the Griller String Quartet. The last wore RAF uniform and had shocking colds. Their long, loud sniffs enthralled us and between each movement they seized their handkerchiefs from the floor and trumpeted into them. Musicians and lecturers endured dreadful train journeys, comfortless delays and draughty halls to bring some beauty to people. It seems unjust to remember their sniffs.

Black-out and air-raids kept people at home in the

evenings, so most concerts were held in the afternoons. Realising what an effort was made to give us the best, I recall with shame my philistine fury at finding games cancelled and — even worse — a requirement to wear white dresses. We loathed these for the good reason that they were so cold. We couldn't wear much underneath and they became skimpy tight as we grew. Older girls could hardly breathe. Having grudged precious clothing coupons on even one such garment, we all resolved never to get another. The visitors thought we looked sweet on the tiered seats round Big School, little knowing how we envied them, snug in overcoats and gloves.

We might have looked sweet but we did not smell sweet, especially at evening lectures in long-sleeved woollen dresses. Our two dresses bore the brunt of every evening activity for 12 weeks before they could be cleaned. A few girls might have exchanged a dress on a rare home outing, but this was not allowed as it was not possible for everyone. Deodorants were forbidden as "naice" girls did not use them. Our chests-of-drawers were inspected and anything cosmetic confiscated.

I remember Eric Hosking, a naturalist, showing his wonderful wildlife slides. At one point he spoke of the maternal qualities of the partridge, who raises a large brood successfully. Since we had Part 1 and Part 2 on the staff, and a third Miss Partridge had come temporarily, a small titter became a large laugh, to the surprise of the lecturer.

Afterwards I was sent for to meet Eric Hosking. First he asked why the idea of a partridge being a good mother should be so funny, and then said he had seen my parents the week before and that they were well. It was a relief to

144

have first-hand news. Of course we had letters, but with petrol tightly rationed we felt cut off and many of us were hideously homesick. This was not WA's fault: we were uncertain what bombs were doing to our homes, and invasion was a real possibility.

One evening the lights failed when we were all assembled in Big School. There were cheers. We were bidden to stay there till power was restored. More cheers! We always had plenty to talk about and an extra half-hour to gossip in the dark was no hardship. Then arose two splendid music mistresses, Miss Mason and Miss Reynell. Miss M was tiny and stout, and Miss R was statuesque and stout. They could play duets at two pianos if they had just enough light to tell black notes from white. Renewed cheers! Candles were brought and they ascended the stage, to deafening applause, fiddled with the music stools and then played to us, spellbound in the dark, with our eyes fixed on the two candles. They ended with "The Flight of the Bumble Bee". It was the first time I'd heard it and it remains one of my happiest memories.

Noreen Beaumont enjoyed a variety of entertainment during the Forties:

There were many after-school activities which I could share with the teachers and pupils, notably theatre visits relevant to our studies. These included Shakespeare with Laurence Olivier at the Old Vic, Racine at the Institut Français and T. S. Eliot and Christopher Fry at a little theatre. I also went alone to a succession of French films, where I experienced the exciting revelation of the language as a means of everyday conversation. Previously it had been a purely literary medium, something you encountered as print on a page.

The whole school was marched to the cinema to see Shakespeare's *Henry V*. We collected photographs of Laurence Olivier and other film actors from *Picturegoer* magazine. My favourite magazine was *Picture Post*, photo journalism at its best, featuring current events at home and abroad. Sometimes one of my French penfriends sent me a comparable magazine entitled *Noir et Blanc*, in which, as in *Picture Post*, reproduction was entirely monochrome.

The leading newspaper (and the most expensive), *The Times*, gave a price concession to students if a regular order was placed. My parents then ceased taking the liberal *News Chronicle* and took a conservative paper to please me! I used to cut out items for the Current Affairs and French noticeboards at school — that was my responsibility.

My long-suffering mother was persuaded to prepare for the visit of a French girl, who would in turn receive me at her home. When the girl arrived my mother was ill with exhaustion and so was I, having queued in the street to apply for my passport and visa.

Fançoise was a haughty Parisienne, especially scornful of our shabby and ill-equipped tenement, still bearing the marks of aerial bombardments. Paris, of course, was undamaged, having surrendered as an "Open City". English and American visitors were not universally welcome there and I was grateful to my French girl's mother, who showed me the sights of Paris and Versailles, and good-naturedly corrected my spoken French — and my attempts to eat a fried egg with a knife and fork.

John McKay grew up in Brechin, Angus, where he enjoyed playing in and by the river. While hunting for treasure he found his last pearl:

The weir at the Auld Brig o'Brechin is now demolished and this has altogether changed the eastwards river; or does memory not forgive the natural change in any river over 50 years? The water diverted into the lade or mill-stream, ran down through the Tecalemit factory to power its machines and went on parallel to the Southesk as far as Craig's Pool, creating the middle bank between the river and the lade. The middle bank was the playground of Queens Park folk; for me it was a wonderful world of adventure and discovery in those long twilight hours of Scottish summer nights in the 1940s.

The Tecalemit people had fenced their grounds to keep me out, so the middle bank started where the fence ended and went on in many moods past the favoured bathing places. The Spootie, a shallow gravel bed where the smallest children could splash about at the muddy bank — "but mind you don't stand on an eel, for it will cut you with its tail!" I feared the fat, black wriggling eel that could be waiting in the mud between the bank and the gravel, though I never did have one cut me and I stood on them often enough. "And mind you don't stay too late on the middle bank if you are little; you can only get back across the lade when the water is down and shallow enough to paddle across."

Further down the river by a few hundred yards was the Dennies, a deeper hole where bathers could jump in or dive from a submerged Granny Stone. The water was cold and over your head beyond the Granny Stone; so you needed a chittery bite to eat as you sat on the bank after a swim, shivering in the sun, trying to get a tan like Dorothy Lamour or Sabu. Even on sunny days it was cold and I never knew anyone who got a tan that way. Here the older children in the carefree stage between childhood and adolescence could swim, or we could wear our towel as a cape and play out the *Mark of Zorro* along the broad path between the Spootie and the Dennies.

Beyond the Dennies the smell of the sewage plant across the lade meant you were coming to the Muffie. This was a stretch used by grown-ups, where the bank sloped steeply to a deep and dark pool. A mystery of men and young women larking about, in and out of the water; excited laughter, splashing, pushing and touching. Not for children to understand the tensions there, cold peat-brown water mostly and you could hardly see the bouldered bottom even on a sunny day.

The river went on beyond the shallows below the Muffie to Craig's Pool. Here the lade and the river came together again at the end of the middle bank in a fast, deep pool with shelving rocks below the water, by the derelict water-bailiff's cottage on the far bank. This pool was used only by the best or most foolhardy bathers, for the river ran away into even deeper water below Craig's Pool; the rocks on one side and the steep hill of Kinaird Estate on the other saw the river fed with the indescribable outflow of the sewage works and go to an almost unknown world beyond — black, dangerous and beckoning.

I look back in horror at the way I used what I found on the middle bank. (This was long before ecology and preservation were thought of.) There was an endless destruction of eels, and every boy had an egg collection ("but don't take more than one egg in four; birds can't count after three"). Cold, sore feet on the gravel and stones did not stay the continual search for kittybeardies and other small fish ("but not the salmon though there are plenty, for the water bailiff will catch you"). Trees and bushes fell to my knife; you can make a wigwam and a bow and arrow — Geronimo! Or a walking stick or a whistle if you knew how, and none seemed to last more than the day.

Pearl oysters were then in fair abundance, and we were ever in the hope of finding that small pink jewel we all wanted. Mostly they turned out to be brown or black, and not many more than a millimetre in diameter.

I knew all the good places to get to from the middle bank. We could fish with our trousers rolled up and our shoes, with socks inside, looped round our neck by the shoelaces. With none of the tools of the trade it was wise to stay in the shallow water. Sometimes there were dozens of oysters in large beds all tucked together for company in the gravel between large boulders. Some shells were found alone like outcasts, right under the bank where the gravel was deep-set with boulders. And so it was when that last bitter pearl appeared.

It had been a glorious day on the middle bank. We had

been swimming at the Dennies until we were exhausted. As the evening wore on, all but Jimmy Spence and myself had gone back across the lade; Jimmy and I went on down past the island and decided to look for pearls. We had been pearl-fishing all through the summer in groups and alone, with only the tiniest little pearls to show for it. My own collection was some five pearls, most small and misshapen, which I kept at home in a small pill box, taken out for regular inspection.

Our rules were quite simple: we were to pearl-fish the difficult bank between the island and the Muffie. It was not easy there, the water ran deep at the bank and we were always in danger of getting in over our trousers. We agreed to share equally anything we found. For hours there was not a thing to be had, then, suddenly, with Jimmy away down the bank, there it was.

As I opened the shell, a lustrous pink pearl, about quarter of an inch in diameter, stared out at me. I did the usual thing — washed it in the river, then popped it in my mouth for safety. Well, you would never find it again if it fell in the river, would you? Jimmy had seen nothing. Should I tell him? Temptation had never been so bad since the day I found the linnet's nest with only two eggs in it. I took it out and had another look — what a beauty! It must be worth a fortune. Jimmy was coming back along the bank. He had found nothing. I stood there with the prize in my mouth, my heart thumping. But, well, you can't tell a lie to your best friend: a Scout tells the truth.

I showed him the pearl and we both gloated and wondered. The only solution was to toss for it. "Heads I get it and tails it's yours, Jimmy." Up went the coin in an arc that seemed to last for ever. I won.

I could hardly look at Jimmy. At home the pearl went into the pill box and shone out like a star among the other miserable little pearls. I took it out so often to look at that Mum and Dad thought I must be daft. Sadly, I found later that "ye may buy the joys o'er dear", and that the winner does not always get what he wants most in the end. Jimmy never played with me again after that. As I grew up and away from the middle bank, going from high school to university and then to work in England, even the pearl was lost. In the years I was away Mum and Dad probably gave the pill box to somebody; they were always generous and they even gave away my birds' egg collection.

Margaret McDonald found that there was plenty of fun and entertainment whilst she was in the Auxiliary Territorial Service:

We had very little money to spend in the army — privates were paid 1s a day, but as a sergeant I received the princely sum of 5s 4d a day. However, I arranged for half of this to be deducted at source and sent to my widowed mother. As I had been working for Boots before I was called up, they very generously paid me 10s a week throughout the war: this was also paid to my mother. Notwithstanding shortage of funds, we were never short of entertainment because of the Army dances, concerts and sports. We also entertained ourselved by singing everywhere we went. We sang as we walked to work; we sang as we dressed to go out; we sang as we marched or were transported by lorry from one site to another.

Our main day of entertainment was Saturday. Some of us used to go without lunch so that we could walk to Aldershot (about five miles) in order to get to the first show at the cinema. When we came out, we went to a café in Aldershot, where we could get a meal for 1s 6d. We then walked back to Church Crookham, had another meal in the local café, went to the Garrison Theatre for 9d, then home to wash and change and on to a dance until midnight. By that time, we were not only exhausted but penniless!

The entertainment in Manchester helped Keith Spooner develop a wry affection for an initially depressing city:

Pubs were the main social focus in Manchester, packed no less on a week night than at weekends, although adolescents had their milk bars. There were large ballrooms, with resident big bands, and smaller "hops" in outlying halls and institutes. But the public bar, known as the Vault, was a male preserve. We stood at the counter with our tankards of mild, bitter or "mixed". If we sat at a table it was usually to play cribbage or dominoes. There might be a small compartment off the end of the Vault, in which would be seated a few middle-aged to elderly ladies with their port wine or bottles of stout.

Most pubs had a Singing Room, sometimes the size of a village hall, with a stage for piano and drums. As the evening progressed booze-enlivened men and women would go up to bawl into the clock-sized microphone.

Sometimes a raw, untutored but genuine talent would hold the room spellbound. The evening ended with the National Anthem, to which everyone stood. Violence, drink-sparked, might erupt, but these altercations were usually on a man-to-man basis, the antagonists taking off their jackets and stalking into the yard outside to settle matters, their mates accompanying them to ensure fair play, not to join in. Fists were still the favoured weapons, knives considered the accessories of "dagos" and "wops", guns associated with such places as Chicago.

Whilst the Free Trade Hall, a bomb victim, was being rebuilt the Hallé seasons were held in the Albert Hall. This venue was owned by the Methodists: during a recital given by the great Spanish guitarist Segovia, sounds of a thumping piano and hearty hymn singing arose through the floorboards from a basement chapel, clashing woefully with Segovia's delicate virtuosity. He played on. On Sunday afternoons the Hallé Orchestra, conducted by the dynamic John Barbirolli, gave concerts at Belle Vue before an audience of thousands, and all for two shillings a ticket. Sometimes a lion from the adjacent menagerie could he heard roaring in a bored way during quieter passages in the music.

The Opera House itself in Peter Street staged a larger proportion of plays than music. We often had first-rate Shakespeare, Godfrey Tearle and Edith Evans in *Antony and Cleopatra*, also one of the last of the flamboyant tragedians, Donald Wolfit, as Macbeth. The small but excellent Library Theatre produced good contemporary drama: for instance, a modern version of *Lysistrata* given by Theatre Workshop before it settled at Stratford East.

153

At Kersal, Broughton House was a home for soldiers bedridden since the First World War. To help raise funds, BBC North Region broadcast programmes from Broughton House, and at one such we were entertained by Violet Carson with songs and monologues. She was already famed as the pianist on Wilfred Pickles's radio show, *Have a Go*, but would find even greater fame as the immortal Ena Sharples in *Coronation Street*.

In the late Forties the Trad Jazz boom began — eventually killed by Skiffle and Rock 'n Roll — and I saw Humphrey Lyttelton's Band at the Onward Hall. This venue was also owned by Nonconformists, and thus no alcohol was permitted (I imagine the musicians brought their own), but the glories of New Orleans lifted our hearts as effectively.

I hated Manchester when I first arrived after demob, for I had recently left Trieste in the first flush of an Italian spring, after nearly a year of spiritually convalescing from war. The rainy cosmopolis seemed to dampen not only my exterior person but my spirit, too. Yet I responded more than I realised and by the time I left in 1950 I had come to feel a wry affection for this vital, dour, dogmatic and life-assenting city, appreciating its efforts to throw off the depressing realities of a dubious and soured peace. I have looked back with a certain nostalgia ever since, knowing that I made the difficult transition from war to peace under its gloomy skies, and had weathered the Forties with all their challenges, hopes, disillusionment and tentative progress.

CHAPTER
SEVEN

Health, Sex

War was to have an important influence on the medical profession. Horrific injuries sustained by civilians in air-raids as well as those inflicted on the Forces on active service were to call for a massive investment in research and new techniques. Airmen shot down often suffered extensive burns, and a great advance was made in skin grafting. Others lost limbs and there were great improvements in the manufacture and fitting of artificial limbs.

In 1943 a Dutch doctor, Wilhelm J. Kolef, made the first kidney machine, but kidney dialysis did not become generally available until the Sixties. Also in 1943 penicillin for the first time was produced commercially, although it had been discovered in 1928 by Alexander Fleming.

Hospitals in Great Britain worked under tremendous pressure. Trainloads of wounded would arrive from the war fronts to be added to victims of air-raids, and in addition the hospitals themselves were likely to be subject to bombing. As well as working very long hours, nurses and others had to take their turn at fire-watching, so getting very little sleep.

By late 1941 it was decided that food rationing might deprive children of necessary vitamins, so those under two were issued free with blackcurrant juice (replaced by orange juice) and cod-liver oil. Later a small charge was made and when supplies of orange juice ran short schoolchildren and others were encouraged to collect rose hips from the hedgerows, for which they were paid 3d a pound. The syrup had a high vitamin C content and so many hips were collected that it became available generally. The health of the nation benefited from reduced sugar and fats and the need to extend the minute meat ration with vegetables. Bonny babies were the norm.

The Beveridge Report was issued in December 1942 and was to form the basis for much of the welfare legislation introduced after the war. The Health Service came into being in 1948. The original estimates for 1948-9 were £150 million but so many were seizing the opportunity to get spectacles and dentures for the first time that the following year it rose to £460 million. To help cover the deficit in 1949 a charge was made for prescriptions.

Great advances were made against tuberculosis, venereal disease and malaria by the new United Nations World Health Organisation. They planned to vaccinate 15 million people against tuberculosis in their first 18 months.

Not surprisingly, there was a large increase in sex-related diseases such as gonorrhoea and syphilis during the war. Men were posted overseas for long periods and at home young girls and some married women had flings with members of the Armed Forces, especially the Americans. The latter had a much higher rate of pay than the British and were lavish with gifts of nylon stockings, chocolate and suchlike. Many happy marriages followed but also many deserted wives and unwanted babies. The illegimitacy rate doubled to 10.5 per 1000 over the war years, reaching a peak of 16.1 in 1945. To these must be added the many illegal abortions.

In 1947 the War Office offered the following advice:

"*Venereal Disease* — If you have ever suffered from any form of this disease be sure that you have completed the treatment and observations recommended by your medical officer; the observation period for gonorrhoea is a minimum of three months and for syphilis two years. Remember that disappearance of signs and symptoms does not mean that you are cured. If you are not really cured you may transmit your disease to others, particularly your wife and children, so for their sakes as well as your own, make sure. If you are in the least doubt go to your own doctor or to one of the many treatment centres situated in most of the larger towns where you will receive advice free and in confidence."

Grace Horseman had to improvise some First Aid remedies in her capacity as personnel officer:

When I qualified as a personnel and welfare officer, I did not fully appreciate all that that would mean. At G. N. Haden & Son in Trowbridge, Wiltshire, I was the only personnel officer. I had an assistant who helped among other things with First Aid, but I had overall responsibility. We had a doctor who visited the factory some days, but nor as frequently for the night shift.

As well as work for the Admiralty, Hadens were allowed to continue with some of their copper department, where there were young apprentices. When girls who were called up were directed to work at the factory most were involved with machinery, but one or two found their way into the copper shop. To help in shaping tubes there was a large vat of hot resin. One bright lad asked a girl to put her finger in to see how hot it was. She did, and as soon as she extracted it the resin solidified, and she came to the First Aid department for help.

This was a new one on me and I could only think of putting her finger in surgical spirit. It worked! Next time it was worse. Someone got another girl to put her whole elbow in the resin, and half her arm was covered. The doctor happened to call but he said it was too dangerous to remove the resin as doing so would take all the skin off her arm. However, after he had gone the girl was so embarrassed that she agreed to try surgical spirit. It worked perfectly, with no ill effects: I was very relieved.

With so many young girls directed to work away from home, it was not surprising there were problems when the

158

British servicemen, and later the Americans, camped in the area. There were few entertainments available for them, apart from the local cinema, so when we were arranging firm socials, dances and other activities I phoned the officer in charge to invite a number of their personnel to join us. The girls were glad to have partners. The servicemen were appreciative and mostly well behaved, but in the wartime atmosphere it was inevitable that one or two girls would be tempted by the more affluent lifestyle of the Americans and the nylons and chocolate they lavished on them.

I was most inexperienced in sexual matters, and was shocked when my assistant said one day that she thought a girl I will call Jane was pregnant. Normally she gained large bonuses on the capstan machine she worked, but that had disappeared recently and she showed slight signs of a bulge.

The next day Jane came to the office to ask if she could go home as she was not feeling well and had stomach pains. I asked if she had a problem, but she said No, so I let her go. Next morning we heard she had given birth to a baby. She claimed to have known nothing about it, had made no preparations or warned the householder where she was living. Fortunately the father married her a few weeks later and as far as I know all was well.

The other case was more tragic. Betty (as I will call her) had met an English soldier while he was stationed locally and her mother frequently invited him home for a meal with them: he and Betty were good friends and he proposed to her. When he was to be sent overseas he persuaded her to see him off. On the way he told her he was a married man, and raped her. She told no one until later, and then I helped arrange a hospital bed for her. She and her mother had agreed to keep the baby and even though the little girl turned out to have spina bifida Betty was determined to look after her.

She stayed at the hospital and with great difficulty managed to feed the child. In spite of all her efforts the baby died a few months later, and we could only feel glad for her.

Wartime led to an increase in diseases such as TB, and the influx of "foreigners" into country districts, as children were evacuated from cities such as Glasgow, brought other infections. Muriel Lees and her family, who lived in Moffat, Scotland, experienced some of these:

I began school in 1940 and the following year developed scarlet fever. I spent seven weeks in an isolation hospital at Lochmaben, and my parents were only allowed to see me through the window for fear of passing on the infection. I had huge blisters on my feet and all my finger- and toe-nails were removed, as I had septicaemia. My friend had diphtheria and spent three months in bed.

All the big houses in town were taken over by the Army, and the surrounding area was used as a training ground. Polish troops were stationed there, too. Those who had a spare bedroom and could accommodate an army officer were paid sixpence per night. Moffat also had lots of evacuees from Glasgow.

There were outbreaks of head lice, and the treatment was

to get your head soaked in paraffin. Those who developed scabies had to go to a special centre, get stripped off and be painted with benzodrate.

In 1946 my father died of tuberculosis. The only treatment that was thought to do any good was fresh air. My father spent exactly a year in bed. Only once, on New Year's Eve, did he get up and my mother carried him downstairs on her back. He had been in the sanatorium but was told there was no hope, so decided to come home. He was only 43. Two other men in our drive died that week, also with TB, and they, too, were in their forties, with four or five children.

I remember my father's funeral — at least, I saw the hearse and cars going up the drive. Women did not attend funerals in Scotland in 1946 but were taken to see the filled-in grave afterwards. I also remember my father's body lying in his coffin in the bedroom for three days, and neighbours coming to look. It was the custom.

Although Margaret McDonald found that health on the whole was good whilst she was in the ATS, there were some things that shocked her:

There were very few problems with health in the ATS. Fortunately, as drugs were never available, the worst problem was unwanted pregnancies. It was amazing how well the girls concealed the fact until the last minute, carrying on with their duties and with regular drill and exercise. The doctor in charge of our platoon, and also of the married families, was a very elderly retired surgeon.

He had been decorated for carrying out operations on the battlefield in the First World War and confided in me once that it was very difficult to be interested in coughs, colds and measles after that kind of experience.

He drove about in an equally elderly car, which had its advantages. He lived in a private house a few miles from the camp, and the married families were apt to ring him up in the middle of the night if their child had a temperature. He always expressed complete willingness to turn out but requested that, as his car had broken down, the family should come and collect him. This nearly always resulted in sudden and miraculous cures.

He found Army bureaucracy tedious and, having once had a fire in his office when all his routine returns were burned, he managed to have another one later on when he was being pestered to send in forms he had failed to complete.

When I was working in the Royal Army Medical Corps barracks at Church Crookham, I felt very sorry for the men who had gastric ulcers, as the only concession to their ailment was a special diet, every single day, of mince and rice pudding. Some of the regular soldiers had been trained as pharmacists, but it was a strange, compact system whereby everything was in prearranged mixtures. For example, the remedy for coughs and colds was a mixture known as Mist.Expect.stim. which, in fact, was very effective.

The aspect of health that shocked me most at this time, apart from the occasional syphilis and gonorrhoea, was the prevalence of body lice, known as pediculosis, a condition I had never previously encountered.

Indians have long believed that the waters of the Holy River (Ganges), as it flows through Benares, are a source of healing. Elsie Paget was to discover that scientific evidence supports their belief:

Our friends were greatly interested in recent scientific discoveries. The rock formation on the river floor, west of Benares, is of an unusual quality. It exudes some chemicals that are carried by the flow of the river into and through Benares. They have strong medical qualities, and the remarkable fact is that people who said that the river has healing qualities were right. Experiments proved that some germ-killing properties come from these riverbed rocks.

Cholera germs can live in the earth for seven years, it is said, but not in this water. Many experiments have proved that cholera germs die after a few hours in Benares water.

One day when we were staying at Benares we took a trip up the river in a westerly direction in a boat just large enough to have two storeys, so that, being higher over the water, we could see more. The flow of the water was steady, even and clear. It was remarkably free from debris, etc., but then here it was a specially holy river and said to be at times a healing river. People, particularly from abroad, laughed at this.

We spent some fascinating hours in various river places. Sick people were brought by friends to bathe. Many who were quite fit enjoyed a bathe, too. This was in the upper flow of the river. Further down, sick friends, gently carried, were dipped in the clear water. The only things that floated on the surface were flowers. Loving carers of sick relatives had brought baskets of beautiful blossoms, cut off from the stem, that floated gracefully along.

Further on was a funeral site, where family members or important folk were about to be cremated. First of all, however, their feet were held gently in the Holy River.

CHAPTER
EIGHT

Shops and Food

It has been said that an army marches on its stomach: in wartime food is just as important to the civilian population. Much of our food in peacetime was imported: Hitler knew this and did his best to strangle our supplies by sinking the ships bringing produce to the country. The Government had learnt from near disaster in the First World War; they had plans for rationing, and the appropriate ration books were prepared well in advance of hostilities. Food rationing was first introduced in January 1940, when there was a basic allowance of 4 oz butter, ham and bacon, 3¼ oz cooked ham, and 12 oz sugar. Special arrangements were made for pregnant women, who had a different-coloured cover for their ration books. They were allowed a pint of milk daily, and first choice of any oranges and lemons available. They also had the right to jump the queues which quickly formed when such delicacies were available. Children up to the age of five had a similar ration, and those aged five to sixteen and a half had half a pint of milk daily. Because arable land had been ploughed up to grow crops, there was a shortage of milk. Extra cheese was available for vegetarians and those engaged in heavy manual work.

Meat was added to the list in February 1940, rationed by value and not by weight, so it was possible to buy a much larger quantity of a cheap cut. Offal, sausages, rabbits and such formerly unknown delicacies as melts and skirt were off-ration, so butchers were besieged whenever some became available. Everyone had to register at one chosen shop for the purchase of all goods on ration, which meant that shopkeepers commanded a previously unknown position of authority and respect. Some items disappeared "under the counter", to be available only to favoured customers. However, shopkeepers had their problems, too, as each tiny square representing the particular ration had to be cut out of the book and sent to the local Food Office. Produce was available in the quantity required for the number of customers registered.

As stocks of food increased or decreased, so the ration for each commodity was adjusted weekly. Other items, such as tea, eggs, dried eggs and sweets, were added, and tinned milk, fruit and fish were on a special "points" system.

Lord Woolton was appointed Minister of Food in 1940 and, although he had a very difficult job, was a most popular minister. People felt he was allocating food fairly, and he produced "Food Facts" in papers and magazines explaining why some foods were in short supply, and gave recipes and "Food Flashes" on radio following the 8.15 a.m. news. His years in social work had given him an understanding of people, and a love for them, which they reciprocated.

To compensate for the shortage of imports, people were asked to Dig for Victory. As well as gardens (including treasured lawns), parks, playing fields, and even the grass verges of roads were dug up and vegetables grown. Potatoes, onions, carrots and other root vegetables formed an important part of the wartime diet. Any left-over food or vegetable waste was collected for use by Pig Clubs. Many people supplemented the meagre fresh egg ration by keeping their own chickens. Even children were encouraged to help by collecting nuts, edible berries of all kinds, and especially rose hips. There was an extra allocation of sugar for jam-making. Flocks of sheep could be seen feeding on the grass in parks and on commons.

School meals expanded to cover 1,850,000 children, compared with the peacetime total of 250,000.

In spring 1941 700,000 tons of shipping was sunk and rationing became more severe, with cheese reduced to an ounce a week and jam, marmalade and syrup rationed. Finally, convoys were introduced so that warships could protect vulnerable Merchant Navy ships laden with their precious cargoes.

The 90,000 members of the Women's Land Army did heavy work, sometimes in atrocious weather. Italian and German prisoners-of-war were also used to help on the land. That year office workers and others were asked to give a hand with the harvest at weekends, and in spite of the long hours they were working in very difficult conditions during the week, they were driven to nearby farms, where they worked willingly until dark.

Conditions became even more serious, and soap was also rationed — just 3oz a month, and milk reduced to $2^1/2$ pints a week.

Many factories introduced canteens for their workers, the number rising from 1500 in 1939 to 18,500 in 1945, and they received special allocations of food. British Restaurants, serving simple but inexpensive meals, were established to help those who could not get hot meals at factories or schools. No restaurant was allowed to serve a meal costing more than five shillings.

Wartime food lacked variety, but thanks to rationing and the advice of nutritianists, it was well balanced and shared out fairly. Many people were more healthy during the war than before. When the war ended rations were actually reduced. The USA cancelled Lease-Lend, and the devastated countries on the Continent had to be fed. There was a world shortage of cereals, and the harsh winter of 1946-7 increased the problem. Bread and potatoes were added to the list of rationed food.

Furniture and floor coverings were also subject

to rationing, and utility furniture was manufactured and sold on a points system. Couples getting married were given extra help, but second-hand furniture was in great demand, especially among those who had lost their homes and contents in the raids. Britain might well have been brought to the point of surrender if the Nazis had succeeded in depriving the people of food. Thanks to imaginative rationing and the use of all available resources and manpower, they were frustrated.

Gary Cornford's father was an excellent gardener and so was able to supplement the wartime rations with home-grown fruit and vegetables:

Our big back garden at Chestnut Cottages had a path down the middle leading to the shed and the Anderson air-raid shelter. On the left side was our play area, but the right-hand side of the path was Dad's vegetable plot and definitely out-of-bounds. Dad was meticulous about everything he did: even peeling the spuds, preparing sprouts or slicing beans, as he did on Sundays to help Mum, were done with clinical precision and a razorsharp knife.

In later years when we had the farm, he went hedge "brishing': that is, making proper hedges in his fields by cutting half-way through stems and folding them down and weaving them into their neighbours. For this he used a hooked hazel stick and his hand bill ("amble" in Sussex dialect and the stick was the "billack"). So his garden was, like his hedges, a work of art. Each autumn the ground was dug and manured. After the frosts it was broken down and raked to a fine, even tilth, and the seeds planted. Eventually we enjoyed the fruits of his labour: new potatoes, freshly dug, and peas which we podded, eating as many raw as went into the pot. Both were cooked with sprigs of fresh mint. Sweet baby carrots completed the vegetables to go with the Yorkshire pud, gravy and whatever meat was available.

Salads were the custom for Sunday tea, with cold meat from dinner time (we didn't call it lunch). My favourite part of the salad was our own fresh celery. This grew in trenches and was earthed up as it grew, to give pale, crisp stems, pungent leaves and the root. We fought to get the root with the wonderful central stalks. Usually it was cut in four to save all-out war. Nowadays celery is green, stringy and virtually rootless.

As well as our garden we had an allotment about half a mile away. This was used for bulk crops like potatoes, swedes, cabbages and curly kale. The path to the allotments was lined with bullace (plum) trees, which allotmenteers shared. When Dad was working at the allotment we all went along with our big black pram and picnic. We made a fire on which to boil the kettle for tea and in the autumn picked apples and blackberries. Sometimes we also came back with hazelnuts and wild crab-apples, which Mum made into jelly. The fire was my joy and pride. I have always loved fire, which is perhaps one reason for my taking up pottery at college. On one occasion I "borrowed" matches and lit dry grass, watching the flames run and then stamping them out. Unfortunately one lot ran faster than I could stamp, and I set the hedge alight. Dad beat the fire out with his spade and would probably have beaten me out if Mum hadn't intervened! Dad was a very strong man.

When I was small my parents bought me a wonderful pedal car. It had a canvas hood to raise and lower, battery operated lights, pneumatic tyres and a boot with a lid.

One day Mum and I went to the allotment to pick rhubarb. She was using her walking-stick to push my car and assist my six-year-old legs. We had just reached the roadway to the allotment when a lady came running from her house. "Nora," she cried, "the war is over." It was VE Day. I can remember that moment so clearly. (Of course, I didn't know what was happening in Japan and have no recollection of Nagasaki and Hiroshima, later.) We finally made it to the allotment and filled the boot of my car with rhubarb. Even at great moments in history, life goes on.

In common with most other families in Britain during the war, ration books tended to dominate shopping for Louise Boreham and her Auntie:

More and more of our purchases were governed by rationing. I grew up believing that ration books were an extra kind of currency that had to be taken to the shops. The "sweetie coupons" ensured that the tin had a constant supply of "pandrops" and butterscotch drops, but Auntie had to spin out the meagre meat, butter and sugar allowances. Fresh eggs were a luxury and if, as often happened, one was rotten, it was carefully preserved in a cup and returned to St Cuthbert's Co-operative (the

171

"store") to be replaced. However, we had large tins of dried egg and I used to love the leathery omelettes it produced. Cakes could also be made with it, but they were a bit stodgy.

Auntie used to make peppermint chews with dried milk and some precious sugar, but dried milk diluted with water wasn't very nice to drink. We got fresh milk at school, although we weren't especially keen on that either, as it could be "off" in the heat of summer, or full of ice in winter. At home, mince and tattles were often on the menu, but I hated the bits of gristle; it was probably just as well we didn't know what went into the mincer. Worse still was the stewing steak, which came in gravy with carrots and swedes. The meat was probably from wornout milk cows and, despite Auntie's best efforts, was still tough after hours of cooking. I always had difficulty in chewing and swallowing it and the more my father yelled at me, the more the dreadful stringy lump went round and round in my mouth. Then out would come the well-worn phrase, "Half the world's starving and would love to have a nice meal like that." Needless to say, all I wished was that they'd come and eat it! Tripe was as bad as the stew and I have never eaten it since the war ended. Sometimes we had rabbit casserole and that was lovely, quite like chicken, although I had never tasted such an expensive delicacy then. Some of our precious sugar ration was saved up to make jam or jelly. I loved going to the Clyde Valley for Victoria plums (which were preserved in Kilner jars). In September we set off with a picnic to the country, where we gathered brambles for jelly, but I wasn't too keen on the thorns.

172

Food wasn't the only commodity in short supply. We lived in the middle flat on the third floor of the tenement and every week the poor coalman would toil up the stair with a bag of coal and dump it in a cupboard, which somewhat illogically we called the coal cellar. The kitchen range provided us with heat, hot water and something to cook on. Therefore, it was on all the year. However, in winter the one bag of coal per week would never have lasted and had to be supplemented by the blocks of wood my father got from his place of work. Before the war, the firm had made church furnishings and high-quality shop-fittings, but in the early Forties it was turned over to war work, and made cupboards and other items for offices and billets. Dad used to bring home scrap off-cuts nearly every day and one of those, covered with coal dross, would burn highly satisfactorily for quite a time.

However, towards the end of the war there was a scare that there would be a fuel shortage and Dad decided we should try to store some coal. Although we had the use of a small cellar at the foot of the common stair and two hundredweight sacks were fitted in there, he decided that might not be enough to see us through. Accordingly, the bath was lined with newspaper and the coal piled up in it and neatly covered over with more newspaper and brown paper. Everyone had to make do with a wash-down until the scare was over, and then it took some cleaning to return the bath to its normal purpose.

Rationing continued after the war but my aunt in Canada was allowed to send us food parcels, which typically contained a precious tin of salmon, corned beef, tinned fruit, breakfast cereals, "Jell-O" (jelly cubes), sweets and chewing gum (much to Auntie's annoyance). Postage on these parcels was considerably reduced if only food was in them, but my aunt used to conceal forbidden gifts among the goodies. I was beside myself with glee when a pair of furry slippers was retrieved from a packet of puffed wheat. Naturally, we ate the contents of the packet afterwards. Another year, it was a yellow brushed sweatshirt. Luckily none of our parcels was opened, or we'd have lost the lot.

Food is important to all schoolchildren and was especially so to Isla Brownless and her friends:

Probably we felt the cold worse at school because of food rationing. We weren't actually hungry till later in the war, though we'd have liked a great deal more sugar and butter. Our butter ration was put out in little dishes with our names. The intractable problem, endlessly debated, was whether to have a minuscule scrape of butter each day, or enjoy a mighty splurge, eating it all at a leisurely Saturday tea-time.

Did other school houses have nicknames for their food? We had a pinkish meat which made a delicious casserole known as Elephant Stew. One pudding had a meringue topping like the waves of the sea and underneath was custard with pineapple chunks. The revolting name of Channel Crossing was not meant as an insult. Another favourite was Treacle Drops, suet paste in dollops, deep fried. They had crunchy golden outsides and were delectable with hot syrup sauce. I wish I could remember

174

more of the exotic names which, surprisingly, we recorded in our hymnbooks. As these were our own property, it was the custom every morning in chapel to write the day's date and the name of yesterday's pudding beside the hymn. When someone had been at Wycombe Abbey for several years, her hymnbook was a positive diary of feasts. We were a superstitious lot and dire penalties were supposed to fall on anyone who failed to keep this daily record. When the Americans came, they were much puzzled by what they took to be a complicated code in the hymnbooks!

It was not easy for newly-marrieds to cope with the scarcities and complexities of food rationing, but Mary Horseman found it was a good training-ground for housekeeping:

I was married in 1940 and had already experienced a year of wartime conditions before I had to run my own home. In many ways the shortages were an excellent way to learn housekeeping. We could not afford to buy much so it helped that there was not much to buy. There was only enough meat, for example, for two meals if we stretched it. We could rarely make it up with non-rationed sausages or offal as they, too, were in short supply. If we were lucky we could get enough for one more meal. Cheese was also rationed so we could not use that often, but we did get a little bacon and sometimes, but not every week, one egg each.

I have made a cake with flour, dried egg, margarine and

saccharine (it was pretty awful, though not too bad if eaten straight away).

People wonder how we managed without refrigerators, washing machines, TV, etc. — but we did. It took time as we had to shop frequently for fresh food and wash by hand. We did have electric irons. Both my daughters were born in this decade — 21 months apart. Imagine washing, by hand and using a boiler, 20 or 30 terry-towelling nappies per day, as well as all the other clothes, especially as soap was in short supply. I sent the sheets and towels to the laundry until I had a washing machine in about 1950.

I remember one lady telling me she made rice puddings by swilling out the milk bottles — she used a lot of them, because she had a large family. I must say I was never reduced to that, although I did use every drop in the bottle. We all swopped recipes and hints, and listened to very good Ministry of Food recipes on the wireless.

We had to improvise toys: they were not being made or sold in the shops. Toothbrush handles strung on a cord, for example, made excellent teething rings. We could also make quite a decent doll from worn-out rolled-up stockings (not nylon, of course, but lisle or rayon).

We read a lot — the public libraries were a godsend — and sewed, making do and mending. People became really good at making things into something else, especially clothes for children, as so little cloth was available to buy and was on ration.

CHAPTER
NINE

Religion

When the Blitz began with the attendant casualties, it was natural that people turned to the Church for support and comfort, especially those who had suddenly been bereaved. Congregations increased in churches away from large towns and places liable to be bombed; city congregations declined, although in the early days of the war attendance increased everywhere.

Clergy were exempt from call-up, but many of the younger ones volunteered to act as chaplains to the Forces. This meant that the older men left at home had a greatly increased workload. One parish priest found himself taking six services every Sunday; another had to officiate at all the funerals in Lancaster, which meant cycling to three different cemeteries.

Many churches were bombed; some congregations sought shelter in the crypt during air-raids, but often the priest stayed in the church and the congregation stayed with him.

Churches suffered in other ways, as church halls and crypts were used as National Fire Service stations, rest centres, canteens and First Aid posts. Black-out was another problem. Many churches held their "evening" service at 3 or 3.30 p.m., but others managed to find ways of covering lights or erecting black-out and so kept to 6 p.m. Such was the intense desire to hear the latest news, especially in critical times, that one vicar installed a wireless and loudspeakers in his church, then invited the congregation to arrive early so as to hear the BBC 6 o'clock news before the start of the service.

The prayer "Preserve us, O Lord, while waking and guard us while sleeping, that awake we may watch with Christ and asleep we may rest in peace" took on an added significance when bombs were falling in the area.

War conditions led to much closer co-operation between Anglican and Nonconformist clergy. Often when one church was bombed, the two congregations would combine, or take alternate services in the remaining building. Others used a village hall or school buildings. Many churches in the evacuation areas were enriched by the presence of new arrivals, and Sunday schools, too, benefited. On War Savings Week an open-air service was held with clergy from all denominations sharing the same platform. Many Anglicans, Baptists, Congregationalists and Methodists held united mid-week services at their churches.

Anglican clergy suffered the effects of clothes rationing. Although a bricklayer and many others could obtain extra occupational coupons, it was considered that a cassock could be worn as ordinary clothing, so the clergy were obliged to part with eight coupons to obtain a new one. This was particularly hard on newly ordained curates.

National days of prayer were held regularly during the war; that on 26 May 1940 was the most impressive, but they were also held on each anniversary of the outbreak of war. However, not all among the local mayors, Home Guard, ARP workers, Guides and others who attended had faith in what was happening. Some felt it was right to pray for victory, others not. It was particularly difficult for Roman Catholics, as the Pope did not condemn Nazi atrocities.

The Edinburgh Conference on Faith and Order in 1937 was attended by 123 churches, but the German Evangelical Church was not represented. Clergy were refused passports by the Nazi Government — an alarming portent of what was to come. However, this and the Oxford Conference did much to cement bonds between Christians from different countries who were soon to be embroiled on opposite sides in the coming conflict.

One important outcome was that a committee was appointed to work out a constitution for a World Council of Churches. The war interrupted their work but contact was maintained between Church leaders in the Allied countries and those in Nazi-occupied territories. Preparations for the inauguration of the World Council of Churches went ahead rapidly as soon as the war ended. It was inaugurated in 1948 at Amsterdam, with representatives from 147 churches representing 44 different countries. Russia was suspicious and would not be involved, nor would the Roman Catholics or some of the ultra-conservative Protestant groups. The headquarters of the Council was established at Geneva.

The "free" churches had no inherited income like the Church of England, so the members of chapels knew it was up to them to provide for their minister's stipend and they expected to tithe their income to support their church. Over the years the Anglican Church had relied on its rich investments, but in time these had greatly decreased, partly because of inflation. The Archbishop of Canterbury, in his Challenge to the Laity, wrote in 1947 that efforts should be made to bring all stipends up to a maximum gross figure of £500 a year.

After ordination a deacon would probably earn £300 a year, a priest probably about £430 a year, plus an official residence (which often was much too large and expensive to run). A car was often essential to his work, and there were many other unavoidable expenses. Unless he had private means that meant a very frugal lifestyle for himself and his family. No one was likely to enter the priesthood for financial gain.

During the latter part of the war congregations had begun to dwindle. With demobilisation and the return of men from overseas there was an increase in church-going, but some men had become disillusioned when in the midst of battle, whilst others had found a faith for the first time. Tubby Clayton's Toc H had reached out to men during the Second World War as they had in the First. Many country churches had been revitalised by the influx of refugees, whilst in others the congregation decreased. Many had lost their homes and could not return to their former churches, even if they were still standing.

Isla Brownless was helped by the Christian atmosphere at her school. At university she enjoyed wide-ranging discussions on faith and religion with people of different denominations. She married a Church of England clergyman whom she met at Cambridge:

At school, weekday mornings began with a ten-minute service in chapel and most evenings ended with brief prayers in our houses. On Sundays there was a chapel service with lovely music and often inspiring preachers. I remember Pastor Niemöller's intensity and the urgency of his message, although I cannot recall a word he said. We were lucky to have truly Christian headmistresses who took their chapel duties seriously. The end-of-term service always included the reading from Philippians 4:8 about "whatsoever things are lovely, whatsoever things are of good report . . . think on these things." What inspiring words with which to send youngsters out to an unknown future! We accepted these religious observances as part of the routine of life and valued them, since wartime routine was liable to suffer a thousand interruptions.

While life was often grimly serious, our feelings were not. Sometimes it was painful containing our giggles. My friend's surname was Jordan and all her neighbours tried to tread on her toes as we sang "When I tread the verge of Jordan", while she tried kneeling on her chair to keep her feet out of harm's way. At prayers in our housemistress's sitting-room the stalk of a tomato, looking like a fat spider, could be dropped close to a friend who — with luck — would utter a squawk when her devoutly closed eyes opened. Nevertheless, these times were oases of refreshment which strengthened us.

At university each of us had to decide his or her own path: college chapel was voluntary and many diversions competed for our time. The Christian societies seemed to me to be all-devouring and I fought shy of them. However, religious, moral and ethical discussions were prominent in our lives, and endlessly did we debate every topic imaginable. Whatever subject we were studying, theology seemed to impinge upon it. Plenty of people tried denying God's existence but I rather think the majority accepted it, while hoping He would keep his place in the background. It was easy to be cerebral about the Almighty but the thought of his intruding into our lives in a personal way was very different and rather alarming.

The Church of England was numerically strong but frail in belief unless at the extreme ends of the spectrum, very high Anglo-Catholic or very low Protestant. Bishop Kirk had recently remarked on this in a splendid truism, "When people don't go to church, it's the Church of England they don't go to." Certainly the Roman Catholics were the best taught and best organised denomination, regularly rounded up and kept up to the mark. I had a Roman Catholic boyfriend and went around with a lively and devout bunch who took their religious observance seriously.

At RC churches the service was then in Latin, and the prayers in English regularly included one for "heretic England". I nearly leapt off my knees in astonishment the first time I heard it! No RC was allowed to attend a service at a church of another denomination. For a very special occasion he (or she) would have to get clearance from his (or her) confessor, probably the all-seeing Father Gilbey. No RC would dream of missing Sunday Mass or of eating anything beforehand: the consecrated elements must be the first food to pass his lips. At a Saturday-night ball, supper would be at 11.30 p.m., and first to the buffet were always the RC undergraduates so they could finish eating before the clock struck 12.

A mixed marriage then meant partners of different beliefs, not different races. All non-Catholic partners had first to be "prepared" at classes with the priest, in the hope that they would convert to Catholicism. The pressure was strong: if the partner did not become an RC, the shortened marriage ceremony was not followed by the Nuptial Mass, and the RC Church made it clear there was a good deal wanting in this union. The non-Catholic partner had anyway to promise that all the children would be brought up as Roman Catholics.

Luckily my RC boyfriend's ardour waned as mine did. Later, as I contemplated marriage to an Anglican priest, I

183

had much to learn about the C of E. What an odd institution it is! As a vehicle for conveying truths about God it is inadequate and yet it has achieved great things. Some of the clergy are quietly heroic and others are among this world's oddest oddities.

The National Health Service, born in July 1948, marked a tremendous change in the life of ordinary parishes, a change as imperceptible but as powerful as a changing tide. Since earliest times, the Church has spotted needs and tried to meet them: hospitals, schools and orphanages begun by the Church were gradually taken over by the State.

Before 1948, the parish had been the network of support, the means of communication and the meeting ground of a class-divided society. The parish priest was often the first person approached in any difficulty, whether of health, money, family, housing, employment or brushes with the law, as well as spiritual matters. This led to a sometimes authoritarian stance by the Church and a corresponding dependency by the people.

My husband, as one of three curates at St Mary's Prittlewell, Southend-on-Sea, went every Monday morning to a staff meeting. The vicar gave them their orders for the coming week and each came away with a list of homes to be visited, including any where there was need or distress. England was being rebuilt after the war and the huge housing estates contained *nothing* but houses. Having foreseen the need for meeting places, the vicar had put this to his parishioners. They dug deep in their pockets; land was bought and two church halls were built for services on Sundays and clubs and social gatherings on weekdays.

The curates ran the Scouts and other organisations until local leaders emerged. Most people were "incomers" without local relatives, so the chuch became the social and religious centre of each area. Naturally the vicar or the curate became a trusted friend and adviser.

After 1948, town halls and social workers took on many of the tasks that formerly faced the parish priest. The people's growing independence of the priest, as his former role was eroded, led him to reassess the balance of his work between the spiritual and practical sides of his job. The Church has had to do this for centuries and the late Forties may come to be seen as a somewhat uncomfortable transition time.

Noreen Beaumont felt isolated as a Catholic for many years:

The Catholic Society, which I eagerly joined when I came to University College, Southampton, in 1947, turned out to be a small fringe group. For historical reasons Catholics were under-represented in State education at a high level. The local churches I attended were largely immigrant Irish. At that time they were obsessed with being "different", a characteristic I have since come across in other immigrant groups. For instance, I embarrassed my landlady and myself by announcing just before a meal that I would not be eating meat as it was a Friday. She hurriedly changed the menu to fish for no less than six of us at table, under which I wished I could have hidden.

Despite kindnesses from local Catholics and others, I felt

isolated. I had the recurrent conviction that I was in the wrong place, which persisted until, 20 years later, I found myself in Ireland and did some inter-Church work for peace. I couldn't see the connection between my father's traditional easy-going Irish Catholicism and what I was studying at college, until I began to read authors of the French Catholic Revival, under the guidance of a Catholic lecturer. Once I had recovered from the shock of hearing unfavourable criticism by a Catholic of books by Catholic authors (how could a Catholic novel be *bad*?), I began to think for myself in a wider context than before.

Having taken a short holiday in Dublin with my father, and two longer visits with a family in a French village, I perceived that Catholics behave more naturally in a country where they are not in a minority.

CET's first experiences of religion were hardly encouraging for a small child, but fortunately her ideas changed as she grew older:

My parents were strictly religious (Plymouth Brethren) and there was much emphasis in the church on the second coming of Christ. Long conversations on this topic took place round the fireside. We were supposedly entering the Great Tribulation, and Hitler was believed to be the anti-Christ. My parents were anticipating the rapture, when Christians would be miraculously removed from the earth as Jesus came as a "thief in the night". I found this thought terrifying, as I was afraid of being whisked out of my bed at midnight. At other times, when my parents were not around and everywhere seemed strangely quiet, I feared that they had been raptured and I had been left behind as I was not good enough to be taken.

I heard a lot about the number of the Beast, and the martyrs who whould be beheaded during the Great Tribulation. Whilst I wanted to do something wonderful, I certainly dreaded the idea of being beheaded in the time of great sorrows. Martyrdom was not part of my desired programme! Possibly this eschatological emphasis was encouraging for adult Christians at that time but, as a child, I found it detrimental; it fed fear rather than nurturing faith.

In addition to these fireside conversations was something very practical which seemed to link with this teaching. Mother had a small green case packed for me, which contained a change of clothes and a few groceries. When I asked for an explanation, my mother, who used to speak in riddles, said, "My dear, we live in such dreadful times — we need to be ready and prepared in case the Lord comes back in the night." I could never work out why the Lord wanted me to have my bag at the ready! In later years I realised that it was for a quick escape or a sudden evacuation.

My father was one of a small group of local preachers who regularly took services in small village chapels. He generally travelled by bicycle. This could be hazardous during the war; on dark, wet, moonless nights, he sometimes ended up in the ditch and would return home indignant and mud-splattered.

The few faithful chapel adherents were mainly elderly women. They all sang the old hymns lustily, accompanied by the squeaky harmonium played by any willing volunteer, irrespective of how well she played it. Hymns such as "Shall we gather at the river?" from the old red Sankey's hymnbook were firm favourites.

These chapels were heated by old anthracite stoves, which would billow smoke at regular intervals, causing dead flies from the rafters to rain down on the unsuspecting congregation. These buildings were inevitably decaying and have long since been demolished.

Harvest Festival services were memorable, as the few countryfolk made the chapels resplendent, decorating them with flowers, fruit and foliage in every conceivable space. Often we were given flowers from the chapel, usually for my sick mother — daffodils, sweetpeas, roses, lupins, chrysanthemums, each in their own season. We also had a variety of fruit and vegetables bestowed upon us at different times from the gardens of these kindly country-lovers.

At the end of the war, a group of local Christians arranged for a week's tent campaign to be held in the small town where I lived. It was known as the "Faith for the Times Campaign". To my delight there were even children's meetings, which I was permitted to attend. It was at one of the adult tent meetings that I made my commitment as a Christian. The fact that I had prayed, asked Jesus into my life, and written out a "Decision card" made me very excited. I skipped all the way home and devoured sandwiches with home-made strawberry jam for my Sunday tea. My commitment was very meaningful to me, and as a result in adult life I have been a firm believer in childhood conversions.

188

The Christian background of his early years at school was to instil a faith in John West that would never leave him:

The years at Christ's Hospital, with school chapel every morning and twice on Sundays, and house prayers every evening, imbued me with the feeling that God was in his heaven and, if all was not right with the world, it was our fault, not his. This has remained with me throughout my life. There was also encouragement from contacts with the Officers' Christian Union at Sandhurst and afterwards, and with the army chaplains in bringing together the Christian and military ways of life.

There was certainly encouragement from George VI who, in the foreword to the pocket New Testament for the Forces, 1939, wrote, "To all serving in my Forces by sea or land, or in the air, and indeed to all my people engaged in the defence of the realm, I commend this book. For centuries the Bible has been a wholesome and strengthening influence in our national life, and it behoves us in these momentous days to turn with renewed faith to this divine source of comfort and inspiration."

It was not possible to hold large church parades in the desert, where Sunday was a normal working day like any other, but there were regular small services of Holy Communion.

On returning to Cairo the Sunday evening service at the Anglican Cathedral was a must. The congregation, mostly servicemen, was so large that there had to be two services, one following the other, and each filled to capacity. Bishop Gwynne in his seventies presided. He had been a missionary in his time and was an inspiring preacher and warm personality. He frequently quoted from Romans, "If God be for us, who can be against us?"

Spiritual values were to the fore in those war years, and there was strong support on the home front. In February 1945 I, together with other servicemen on the parish roll, received a letter from the vicar and churchwardens of Kingsdown, Deal, preparing the way for our return, and saying, "We would like you to know that you have not been forgotten by the parish, either by prayer or thought, and your name has been mentioned each week in church." The same would have happened in most other churches of all denominations.

Philip Brownless recalls attitues to religion in the Forties. After the war he was accepted for ordination and went to Ridley Hall theological college:

When the war broke out in 1939 I was 19. A minority of the country, as today, was Christian but nonetheless the Church had a widespread influence on most people's lives. National days of prayer and certainly the inspiring talks by Archbishop Temple in factories, universities and many other places had the effect of heightening religious feeling during the war.

A few months after the war had begun I said goodbye to Selwyn College, Cambridge, and joined an infantry regiment. There were a number of church people in my company, but most soldiers were not interested. Few were hostile, though there was some feeling against church parades. There were some excellent chaplains, but the job was a difficult one and many could not cope adequately in wartime. Fancy wasting a valuable padre's hour with young recruits talking about various old standards and artefacts of the regimental chapel! More help and training might have been given. After the war the newly set up Chaplain's Depot at Bagshot helped to remedy this. Compulsory church parades were still in order, and I remember a sergeant-major in the middle of a service telling a soldier, "When you are in church you will bloody well behave!"

One of the more encouraging things about the later Forties was the number of excellent and experienced men coming out of the services who offered themselves for ordination. The theological colleges were full of men who had experienced the dangers and difficulties of war: they expected to work hard when they served in the parishes. Most were acutely aware of the social problems of the time — and perhaps over-concerned to justify their existence. The Church struggled hard to provide a presence and amenities in the vast new housing estates. The 1662 Prayer Book, used with imagination, still sufficed, but only just. There were rumblings about the monotony of repeating the same old prayers every Sunday. Moffatt's translation of the New Testament and the books of C. S. Lewis were very much in vogue.

Relations with the Roman Catholics were very different from today. I was saddened the first time I led nurses and other staff singing carols round the wards of the large municipal hospital on Christmas Eve. We arrived at the end of the evening in the large entrance hall for the last carol and before I, as an Anglican priest, said a prayer and gave the blessing all the RC nurses scuttled off down the passage. They were not allowed to stay.

With Hindus and Muslims as well as Christians living in the same area, Elsie Paget experienced some of the difficulties this caused in Raniganj:

Raniganj had a Leper Home and an industrial school where the untainted children of lepers could live and be educated and learn trades. What a happy place it was! A hibiscus hedge two feet wide and up to three feet high surrounded the Leper Home, so that children and friends could converse frequently and safely with their leper relatives and friends. Raniganj had many Muslims, Hindus and a few Christians. There was no large church but all had some place of worship. The small church and the Leper Home church were my husband's responsibility, along with his other duties in the area.

Usually the various groups lived peacefully together. However, there were occasions when feelings ran high. This might be when a Hindu procession, cheerfully walking through the town, allowed one of their people to throw some Holy Water over a group of Muslims. Sometimes a few shouts, or fists, smoothed it over but on one occasion a riot broke out and a number of people were hurt. These were mostly young men who were only too glad of an excuse for a fight. Many had to go to the hospital, which was run by a Hindu committee. Here there were some house-helpers with one or two trained nurses.

The matron was a Christian (a widow, which of course reduced her status).

The weather was very hot, and Mrs Das, the matron, was anxious. The doctor was a Hindu and Mrs Das tried to get equal care for all patients. This was difficult. She worked very long hours and inspired her helpers. Most patients recovered and Mrs Das saved many Muslim lives, but a few had wounds that turned gangrenous.

At the end of it all, the committee told Mrs Das to go. They no longer had any use for her. Fortunately she had one son, grown-up and at work in another town. This, in Hindu eyes, made her completely respectable.

To our delight, a Christian hospital in another town offered Mrs Das the post of matron, and she settled there very happily. Many, many prayers had surrounded her.

While night-watchmen were not necessary everywhere, Raniganj was a place where it was wise to have one: he was called a "chokidar". He was from Nepal and rested by day and came each evening. He was armed with what a friend called his "Snickershee" — a double-bladed, foot-long, broad knife. Happily he did not need to use it, except to cut tamarisk branches to help me decorate the church for Christmas, which he much enjoyed.

Juliana Ray was living in Hungary when she discovered a faith that was to sustain her during the terror that followed:*

* Adapted from *By Grace Alone: An epic journey of faith through three generations of a Jewish family* by Juliana Ray, published by Marshall Pickering, pp. 73-8.

A few months after my marriage to George he was confined to hospital following an accident, so I was left to complete the furnishing of our flat on my own. The firm that had supplied my furniture sent along a woman whom they said was a specialist in making the loose covers that I needed for protecting the upholstery in summertime (as was customary in Hungary). She was Polish, but we were able to converse in German. While she was busily cutting the material she started chatting. "You are Jewish, I believe?"

I was taken aback by this directness.

"You have a lovely flat," she commented and then carried on, "a great collection of books, too; do you have a Bible?"

This I found more bizarre. After all, religious matters are private. This woman was a bit too inquisitive, I thought. "No," I admitted.

"Oh, isn't it sad," she said, with real sincerity in her voice, "a daughter of Zion and yet she does not know her own scriptures."

Daughter of Zion? What an odd but lovely way to describe a Jewess. She put down her work and started to tell me about herself.

She was a Gentile who had married a Jew in Poland; at present she was sharing the fate of her Jewish husband and had come as a refugee with him after Hitler's occupation of Poland. From her story I realised that her predicament was worse than mine, yet she radiated peace and joy. When I questioned her about the source of her optimism she spoke of the love and care of God for mankind and for each of us, his children. This sounded absurd to me. God, loving mankind? God, loving me personally? I could not see much sign of it.

She explained that cruelty, persecution and war are the consequence of sin. God gave us all free will; it is his most precious gift. When we use it for evil instead of good we cannot return the responsibility to God for the outcome. But God has not discarded us, he still loves us and is with us in all our griefs and sufferings.

I still could not see what comfort this could be and asked, "What proof do you have that what you say is true?"

Then, for the first time in my life, I was presented with the good news, the Gospel, as a reality. I could not accept it all and asked many questions, which she answered with such authority that I was convinced she not only believed them but "knew".

Before leaving, she said, "You don't have to accept what I tell you, start to read the Bible, the Old and the New Testaments, and think about what you read and judge for yourself."

She finished her work and left me with a friendly smile. I have never seen her again. Her name was Mrs Schaffer. Most likely she disappeared in one of the concentration camps.

I would have forgotten this episode in all the turmoil of our life but it was meant to be otherwise. For some time I had planned to take English lessons; a good friend of mine had recommended an English teacher, but had warned me that "she is one of those believers". That aroused my curiosity and I met Mary Majos. Soon I met her husband Emil, too, originally an orthodox Jew but now a Christian, who knew both the Old and the New Testaments well. They invited me to attend Bible studies held both in their home and in a Lutheran church. I argued, debated and questioned everything but, following their advice, started to read the Bible and interpret it for myself. In the end it was neither Mary nor her husband but the written word that convinced me. I read all the Gospels first, looked up references to the Old Testament, read the prophecies and finally came to the point when I had to ask myself: was Jesus, of whom the Gospels draw such a perfect yet realistic portrait, a dreamer, a madman or a false prophet? If he was none of these, then I must believe that what he said of himself was the truth.

Eventually, I began to feel sure of my convictions. Of course, I would have loved to share them with George but there was hardly any opportunity for this while he was in hospital, because we were never alone. However, at last he was permitted to leave the hospital temporarily. For the first time we could move into our flat. His accident had been in March, 1943 and it was now November.

When we had settled down I brought up the subject, carefully and cautiously, knowing that George was something of an agnostic. However, I found him more pliant than I had anticipated. "I confess," he said, "that during many sleepless nights in the hospital I often asked myself what life was all about and why there was so much suffering and injustice in this world. Is there a God at all? If so, does he care for mankind, or do things happen without any preconceived order or plan?"

When he shared these thoughts with me I ventured further and asked him to come along to Bible study with me. He was hesitant. "I'll tell you what, my dear, I'll come with you once, for your sake and to show that I am not altogether antagonistic to what you now seem to believe. However, if I find that this philosophy is not to my way of thinking, promise me that you won't insist on my attendance in future." I promised.

An occasion arose quite soon. Mary and Emil, who knew George only from my account of him, prayed that the Holy Spirit might touch him at the first encounter. He did not say much about his impressions. It's not his style. But he came again next time, without comment.

Christmas 1943 arrived and for the first time it was *our* Christmas. George and I went to buy a little tree, decorated it and on Christmas Eve sat in candlelight and sang together some of the hymns we had learned, feeling a real affinity with other Christians throughout the world.

In January 1944 I came to a decision: I wanted to be baptised. I wanted to belong to the "body of Christ". I believed that in the Church there was a place for both Jew and Gentile, also that if I wanted to enter into this united body I would have to commit myself to it. I knew it would not change my Jewish identity, neither in myself nor from the point of view of recent legislation, which was based on racial rather than religious discrimination.

Mary and Emil arranged the ceremony in a Lutheran church and we combined the occasion with a blessing on our marriage, so far legalised by the civil authority only. It was a simple yet moving service. Only Mary and Emil, Shari mama (my mother) and Ilonka mama (George's mother) were present. Our two dear mothers were unable

197

to share our spiritual experience but would not have missed an occasion so precious for their children.

The reaction to our "conversion" was very mixed in the family. The greatest opponent was my sister-in-law Edith, who was shocked by it, and we had many discussions that led nowhere, of course. However, a few months later she, too, came to believe in Jesus. My parents accepted that we had chosen a different path; whatever they may have felt, they certainly never expressed bitterness or resentment.

CHAPTER
TEN

The Armed Forces and Their Impact

In May 1940 Members of Parliament at Westminster called for Chamberlain's resignation. On the 10th he was replaced by Winston Churchill, who headed a National Government. Also on 10 May Germany invaded neutral Holland and Belgium, and as there were fears that France was to follow, there was mass evacuation.

The speed of the German advance stunned everyone, and the British Expeditionary Force had to be evacuated from Dunkirk. Many small boats belonging to fishermen and others joined the Royal Navy in bringing most of the men back under fire, some boats making several journeys.

As the Germans overran France, Marshal Pétain, France's leader, asked for an honourable cease-fire on 17 June. The south of France remained independent and was governed from Vichy; the rest of the country was occupied by the Germans. The Channel Islands were also invaded, the only part of the British Isles to be occupied by the Germans.

Hitler cynically marched against his ally, Russia, in June 1941. Taken by surprise, the Russians suffered heavy losses but resisted stoically, millions dying in the siege of Leningrad.

America had been helping Britain through Lease-Lend, but was not willing to commit her forces to combat. However, when the Japanese attacked Pearl Harbour, Hawaii, the USA could remain neutral no longer and declared war on 8 December 1941, becoming a member of the "Grand Alliance", together with Britain and the Soviet Union.

In 1942 the Nazis advanced to Stalingrad, which was fiercely defended by the Russians. Eventually the German Army was surrounded and defeated. Meanwhile British Forces in Africa were engaged in a war against the Italians and later the Germans under Rommel. The Allied Army was forced to retreat into Egypt but then under Montgomery mounted a counter-attack. Rommel was routed at El Alamein in November 1942 and that same month Allied troops landed in French North Africa. In May 1943 the German and Italian armies in the area surrendered.

That summer Allied Forces invaded Sicily, moving up into Italy: Mussolini was succeeded by Badoglio who surrendered in October. The Italians then changed sides. However, the Germans soon sent their troops into Italy and there was fierce fighting before they were finally driven out early in 1945.

Meanwhile, Russia was in full production and

soon outnumbered the Germans in men and equipment. Hitler began an offensive against Kursk in the summer of 1943 but the Germans were forced to retreat. In the Pacific, too, the Allies were gaining some ground against the Japanese and successfully invaded the Gilbert Islands.

The Russians had long been urging the Allies to open up a second front, and preparations had been going on in secret for two years, while the Navy had been taking vital supplies to Russia in appalling conditions and suffering many casualties at sea. On D-Day (6 June 1944) the combined British, American and Canadian forces landed on Normandy beaches. The Allies had made the Germans believe that they intended landing at Calais and took them by surprise. There were no natural harbours, so enormous concrete blocks were prepared and towed across the Channel, making the important Mulberry Harbours.

General Montgomery was in command of the Allied Forces, who suffered many casualties but succeeded in pushing the Germans back. Heavy bombing raids were carried out on German cities, including Berlin, to help the advance. Then Hitler mounted a counter-offensive in the Ardennes, called the Battle of the Bulge; there was a temporary retreat but by the end of December the German advance had been halted.

The first V1 (flying) bombs were launched on London in June 1944. Many V1s were shot down but those that got through caused a lot of damage and casualties. The V2s that followed were even worse: their speed far exceeded that of sound, so there was no warning. The advancing Forces gradually destroyed their launching sites.

At the Yalta Conference in February 1945 President Roosevelt, Winston Churchill and Stalin met in the Crimea to discuss arrangements to follow the defeat of the Germans. Churchill mistrusted Russia, but Roosevelt did not. Britain and her allies approached Berlin from the west and Russian forces from the east. Russians were in Poland, Berlin, Prague and all the East European capitals and they were not going to release this territory. Hitler and others committed suicide on 30 April and the German armies soon began to surrender. Victory in Europe was declared on 8 May (VE Day). The war with Japan continued until the dropping of the atom bombs on Hiroshima and Nagasaki. This led to unconditional surrender by Emperor Hirohito on 15 August (VJ Day). Roosevelt had died three days earlier, so failed to witness the final peace.

Gary Cornford's mother managed to make the war an interesting time for her children so that they were not afraid and enjoyed meeting soldiers:

One autumn afternoon (1943 or 1944, I suspect) we were in the garden when the front gate flew open and soldiers came rushing down the path. To our horror they ran across

Dad's vegetable garden, fell flat and started to shoot their rifles through the hedge towards a hilly area two fields away. Their fire was returned from behind a hedge around the market garden on the hill. We just stood and watched. Mum explained they were on manoeuvres and were not using real bullets. From time to time they would take out large thunderflashes. These did not have blue touch papers, instead they had ends like Swan Vesta matches. These the soldiers scraped on the soles of their boots to ignite and then lobbed them over the hedge.

The first soldier had ended up by the fence at the bottom of the garden and lay in a bed of nettles. Rose (Rosemary) and I were mightily impressed by this. He asked us for a glass of water and we ran indoors. Mum filled a glass and gave us an apple to take as well. This was no ordinary apple. It was from our own tree and was a Charles Ross, which was like a small pumpkin. It must have weighed about 2 lb. When fresh-picked they are fragrant and crisp. This apple bought us a friend and soon we were filling a satchel with all the empty brass cartridge cases from the soldiers' Lee Enfield 303 rifles.

These gave us much fun. Rose, the cousins and I spent happy hours running the gauntlet down the passage from the front door whilst one of us on the stairs above emptied the cartridges from the satchel.

The soldiers in our garden were British. The "enemy", two fields away, were Canadians. One day we found a soldier's sewing pack in the road near the house. We showed it to one of our Tommies. He told us it belonged to a Canadian soldier, so Rose and I, hand in hand, walked the 100 yards up the road. We went to the soldier on guard at the gate of the field and showed him the sewing kit. He took it, looked at the name and number inside, and went off to find the owner. Eventually he returned minus the kit. He said the soldier was very pleased to get it back and would like to give us a present in thanks. Chocolate and chewing gum! The chocolate was wonderful but the chewing gum was something else. We'd never had it before. It lasted and lasted; I'm sure we stuck it on our bedposts on the first night at least.

When the doodlebugs started coming over, we used to camp under the stairs. Mum fixed a blanket up to cover the opening and we ate sultanas, peanuts and raisins, and she read Rupert comics to us until the All Clear sounded. Being in Sussex we had German bombers coming over in waves on their way to London, as well as the V1s and V2s. Hurricanes and Spitfires from Biggin Hill and West Malling would meet them. Polish pilots were particularly fearless and, reportedly, would be like the Japanese "Kamikaze" in that they would fly their planes into collision with the enemy. The German VI rockets were unstable, with their little stubby wings, and the RAF devised the technique of flying alongside them in their Spitfires and edging a wingtip under the wing of the rocket, then tipping it over to fall into Pevensey marshes. Unfortunately the explosion would blow out the windows of houses nearby.

Children could adapt to war more quickly than adults, as did Vivienne Hubbard:

I was almost six when the war broke out, so my memories of it are sporadic. We listened to the planes passing overhead day and night, and we children were soon able to speak knowledgeably about whether the engine sound denoted one of ours or one of "theirs". When I was evacuated I was able to put straight my grandparents, uncles and aunts, who had less experience of these matters in their village. It amused me to see them cower under the table or corner cupboard unnecessarily.

The actual progress of the fighting did not greatly impinge on us beyond the reactions of our elders. When things were going badly, I can remember one teacher being irritable. After the Russian entry into the war I grew accustomed to Dad's shouts of "Good old Joe", before we knew what Joe had been up to back home. We were more affected by the big drive in the kitchen to preserve all fruits that could be saved, especially raspberries and tomatoes in our house.

Once war had been declared, Hungary, as part of the Berlin-Rome axis, had to be prepared to get involved. Laws and regulations restricting the employment of Jews affected thousands of families, including that of Juliana Ray:

At the beginning of the Forties, my father, who ran his own timber business, was allowed to carry on unhindered although he was a Jew, mainly because he had been an officer in the 1914-18 war and had been decorated for outstanding bravery. In fact, work increased as wood came to the timber-yard from forests in territories recently returned to Hungary.

This meant that my mother, Shari mama, had additional secretarial duties in addition to the social work she was doing. However, she was greatly concerned about Bandi, my brother. He had recently married Edith and was now being called up for longer and longer periods, stripped of all previously acquired rank and exposed to rude insults from any sergeant-major who happened to be anti-Semitic.

During this period I met George. I was 17 and he seven years my senior. He had a good job and came from a good family, so our friendship was approved by my parents. Bandi and Edith were very sympathetic and took us out several times in their rowing boat. George was a good oarsman and the four of us went on day-long excursions. One Whit Sunday the men had stopped rowing and we were enjoying the perfect silence of the calm river, far from any town, when we heard church bells calling people to prayer. I experienced the loving, all-embracing presence of God. This was our last outing together with Bandi and Edith. Bandi was called up again to march with the army into Transylvania, now re-annexed to Hungary by the "generous" Germans. George was also called up several times for duty in forced labour camps, introduced especially for Jewish young men who for some reason had no military training.

So came the winter of 1941. This time Bandi's division got their marching orders in the direction of Russia. We made a quick farewell on the platform, waving and crying — and he was gone. Edith was just beginning her pregnancy and we all hoped that by the time the baby arrived Bandi would be with us again.

Times were so uncertain, that my parents themselves suggested that George and I should get married whilst weddings were still possible. Our wedding took place in a register office, followed by a family lunch in a hotel. From there we left to spend our honeymoon in a holiday flat on a nearby hillside and had been there only six days when George's summons to the camp arrived. We rushed home quickly and packed his rucksack.

So George was gone too, and I moved back to my parents' place as if I had not been married at all. Our flat, newly bought and furnished, with all my lovely trousseau and our gorgeous wedding presents, was deserted. I visited it sometimes and hoped that one day we might be allowed to live there.

In October 1942 Tommy was born to Edith and Bandi. Many photos were taken of him and sent to Bandi, who counted the days until he could see him in person. However, his letters ceased after January 1943. The siege of Stalingrad was on and we knew he was in that area.

In March 1943, six months after our wedding, I was visiting a friend when I received an urgent telephone call. It was Shari mama: I should go straight to a military hospital because George had had an accident and had been taken there by ambulance. His labour camp group had been working on a building site and while he was up on some scaffolding it had collapsed and he had fallen from about the second floor on to his back. He had regained consciousness minutes before I arrived at the hospital. He was in agony day and night for two weeks afterwards, yet apart from a daily inspection no nurse came into the room where the Jewish boys were kept. Only when the X-rays showed that George had broken two vertebrae was he given a bed on his own.

At last, George, still encased in plaster, was permitted to leave the hospital temporarily. For the very first time we could move into our flat. His accident had been in March: now it was November. A few relatively settled weeks followed; George's plaster was removed, and a steel corset replaced it during the day. He resumed work in his office in the hope that he would be able to continue there, since he was war-disabled and therefore unlikely to be sacked or called to do any more forced labour.

By April 1944 the country was occupied by Germans. The very first thing they introduced was the yellow star, which had to be worn by all Jews, irrespective of their religion. Even with the yellow star we were allowed in the street only for a few hours each day; anyone found outside after curfew was arrested and never seen again. The Jewish population of Budapest was forced to concentrate in houses marked with the yellow Star of David. Neither my parents' home nor ours had been marked in this way and therefore we had to move out and leave a good deal of our furniture and other belongings behind.

We all crowded in with Edith, whose apartment was in a house marked with a star. It was a squeeze but at least we were all from the same family, without outsiders. My uncle Pali and his family also moved to the same house with some other friends of ours. Altogether there were 15 adults, one baby and Tommy, who was 18 months old. Except for the mothers of the small children, we all had some job allocated to us, to be done during the time we were permitted to spend outside the house.

The news from the provinces was becoming more and more alarming. Edith's parents were put in a train with many others — destination unknown — and so were all Jews, gradually, apart from those in Budapest who were apparently being left until last. The repeated air-raids we hardly cared about. Indeed, during the bombing spells there was no extra molestation for Jews and we all thought that dying quickly during a raid would not be the worst of fates.

Then came the day when all Jewish men and women under the age of 50 had to report to a certain racecourse, from where they would be taken to various destinations. George was the first to leave for the racecourse. In spite of his steel corset he was commanded to go on foot with the other young men to the Austrian border. I was luckier. Because I was a seamstress I was allocated to a group of Jewish women working in a synagogue building. Sewing-machines had been installed and our job was to mend torn uniforms. We were kept there day and night, fed as little as possible, and had to sleep on the floor.

In those critical days Raoul Wallenberg, a diplomat attached to the Swedish embassy in Budapest, initiated a scheme to save as many Jewish lives as possible. The Swedish embassy started to issue protective passports in the hope that those in possession of such papers, issued by a neutral country, would escape the general fate, and the passport would be respected according to international law. This practice was soon followed by the embassy of another neutral country, Switzerland. Protective signs were also issued by the Swedish and Swiss Red Cross organisations and placed on some of the houses previously marked with the Jewish Star outside the ghetto area, hoping that those living there would escape the pogroms that seemed to be inevitable.

The house where my Aunt Manci and Uncle Feri were living became one of those protected by the Swedish Red Cross. It was in Pest, on the other side of the Danube, and my parents and Edith moved in there.

Shari mama was the one who, with her permit to stay out of the house longer, undertook to join the enormous queue until she obtained the protective passport for George. By some miracle the passport reached him, and with it in his pocket he took a chance on escaping from the labour camp during the night. After some trouble he found where my parents were staying. He was now a "deserter" and the problem was where to hide him. Our friends Mary and Emil had a free movement permit, which had been obtained for them by the Calvinist Church, to enable them to work among Jewish Christians. When they heard of George's plight they offered to have us both at their flat.

Mary's and Emil's flat looked like a refugee camp. Mary disguised herself as a Red Cross sister, wearing a big white head-dress and, with the help of a friendly ambulance driver, managed to transport people or bring them from Jewish houses on a stretcher, to be hidden in her own home. The Church commissioned Mary and Emil to find premises and organise homes especially for the care of children separated from their parents or for mothers and babies. Several big houses stood empty, their occupants abroad, and a few were re-opened for this purpose after

210

receiving the protective shield from the Swedish Red Cross.

We went with Mary and Emil when they moved into one of these houses to help run the place. A few other adult workers were also installed and soon the children and mothers started to pour in. Before we knew it the villa was accommodating 150 souls. George looked after the administration of the place while I played with the children to keep them occupied during the day. I, too, wore a white head-dress, like a nurse, with a red cross. When the siege of Budapest began, Mary alone ventured out daily in her uniform, a rucksack on her back, collecting food wherever she could find anything edible and available, then carrying it home for the 150 of us.

Emil and Mary also provided us with our spiritual food. Each morning and evening we read the Bible together and many of the young mothers and the older children came to the Lord in those days. Amongst them was Edith, who had temporarily joined us with Tommy, and we thus came even closer together now that we could share a common faith.

Christmas Eve 1944 was the last night we spent upstairs in the house and we celebrated it as best we could in the circumstances. Next morning, looking out from the window, I noticed that Hungarian Nazi troops had surrounded the building opposite, which we knew to be a Jewish orphanage. All the children and their tutors were dragged out and led away. Horrified, I wondered where they could have been taken now that the Russian army stood at the gates of Budapest and all transportation from the capital had ceased.

We soon got the answer. Shari mama phoned. "My dear," she said, "I have some very sad news for you. Last night the Hungarian Nazis behaved as if all the devils in hell were let loose. They surrounded several protected houses, ignored the Swedish or Swiss protective signs and dragged people out, then drove them to the banks of the Danube, shot them dead, and threw the bodies into the partly frozen river. Some of the women they thought too weak to swim were thrown alive into the icy water, presuming they would freeze to death anyway."

Seven of our relatives were among the victims, but Ilonka mama was thrown into the Danube alive and managed to swim about half a mile until she reached the steps leading down to the river from the Houses of Parliament. She staggered out from among the iceblocks and hid under the dark arcades above the steps. There she was found by a friendly police patrolman, who felt compassion towards the shivering elderly woman and escorted her, wrapped in his cloak, to the Swiss embassy.

The six weeks that followed Christmas were a nightmare. We were all crammed into the cellar; there was no more food in the house; and no civilians were permitted in the streets at all. Gradually we could hear the Russian guns getting closer and closer and the German and Russian soldiers were fighting hand-to-hand in the streets. Then one day our cellar door opened. There, framed by the winter sunshine, stood a Russian soldier. We were "liberated"; our ordeal was over! However, that evening the young Nazi living next door, who had blackmailed us for weeks, now entered the cellar with two Russian soldiers. Wanting to do them a favour, he pointed to the

212

unprotected women. Emil, George and the two other men were to be taken outside and shot.

At this moment our cellar door opened again. This time a high-ranking Russian officer appeared, looking much more civilised, and spoke to us in perfect French. "Ladies and gentlemen, I am the commander of this area and my headquarters are next door. If you have any problems, just call on me." The privates sneaked out the moment the officer appeared.

A couple of days later the cellar door was opened yet again, and there stood Dadi, looking old and unshaven, with Shari mama in tears. When they realised that we were alive, the relief brought more tears from all of us. They were able to inform us about Edith and Tommy, who had been well looked after in their last hiding place and Ilonka mama had recovered and was well, staying with my parents. They heard of other members of the family who had been miraculously saved, whilst so many others had been killed.

Close relatives lost

Name	*Note*
Aunt Erzsi	shot into the Danube
Uncle Arthur	shot into the Danube
Gyriu	shot into the Danube
Judith	starved in the ghetto
Uncle Henrik	shot on the wayside
Zsuzsi	gassed in Auschwitz
Erika	gassed in Auschwitz
Jeno	burnt alive in barracks

213

Imre	died in forced labour
Uncle Lakatos	gassed in Auschwitz
Aunt Lakatos	gassed in Auschwitz
Grandmother	shot into the Danube
Bela	shot into the Danube
Teri	shot into the Danube
Bandi	died in a Russian prison camp

The main problem in the children's home now involved feeding 150 people. I noticed women going to the frozen carcases of horses and carving meat from them, so I did the same. I returned to the home with a huge amount of meat, out of which we made a large pot of soup. "The most delicious soup and meat we have ever had," said the children.

I repeated this exercise every day until the source was exhausted. Then we had to exchange our engagement rings and watches for flour and potatoes brought by the peasants.

Meanwhile the repairs to the house went on as best they could without materials or workmen. The relatives of the children and the mothers began to turn up. What scenes of joy we witnessed every day! Still, much anguish had to be shared with those for whom nobody came. Hope faded for some as the weeks went by. Finally, however, we found homes for all the children and we too moved out, starting a more normal life, first in Ilonka mama's apartment and then later in a flat for ourselves. So circumstances gradually settled: we hoped and planned for a family. In 1946 our first son, John, was born.

As John West's career was in the Army, his occupation and the war were intertwined:

After Sandhurst I was commissioned into the Royal Corps of Signals, although I had originally been heading for the Indian Army. My first posting was as Signal Officer to the 4th Field Regiment RA in September 1940. The regiment was in the Sudan as part of 5th Indian Division preparing for the Eritrean Campaign. During the campaign I was one of the last people to use the heliograph in action. This instrument was developed mainly for use by Army Signals in India, where the sun shines for much of the day. It had a mirror which was aligned to reflect the sun on to the distant station. With the key up, the mirror was deflected into a rest position. Pressing the key brought the beam back to the distant station and it was held down for the period of the dot or dash of the Morse code. With the sun shining, the heliograph had a much longer range than lamp or flag, and it could be used wherever a line-of-sight path was possible. In Eritrea it provided an excellent link to a Sudan Defence Force outpost which could see the Italian-held fort at Agordat, the target for a regimental shoot.

After the Battle of Keren the regiment returned to Cairo to refit, and in June 1941 I was posted to command the Signal Section of 22 Guards Brigade, which was holding the coastal sector of the front line in the Western Desert. The brigade remained in the front line continuously for the next year. During that period the brigade's responsibilities became those of a motor brigade, and in consequence the Signal Section, starting with a strength of 38 men, grew into a squadron 240 strong.

Then, in June 1942 the brigade, by then known as the 201 Guards Brigade, was captured when Tobruk fell, but I was fortunate. I had been visiting a remote radio station which could not get through — no wonder because the far end had been captured, but we were not aware of this. On returning to Brigade HQ I found that they had been overrun and captured whilst I was away. There was nothing for it but to make myself scarce and emerge the next day, when I was joined by two RASC sergeants. Discarding badges of rank and using an abandoned 15-cwt truck, we drove out through the perimeter defences on the main east-west road. In doing so we had the misfortune to join a German 88-mm gun convoy heading east at full speed. However, the fist-shaking Germans seemed more concerned at this breach of convoy discipline than that the offenders might be escaping British. My companions and I also had the novel experience of being protected en route by lowflying Messerschmidt 109s. The Messerschmidt 109 engine had a distinct whine, and we cringed on hearing its approach; but then in relief we said to each other, "It's OK, they're ours!" Once safely through the perimeter we headed south and after a 160 mile detour through the desert we were able to rejoin 8th Army.

Navigation in the desert was easy provided one had a "Barrel" map, and fortunately there was one on the truck we picked up. The Army surveyors had planted numbered barrels at about ten miles apart throughout the desert. I worked out the distance and compass-bearing to the next barrel, drove there, searched and, having found the barrel, proceeded on the next stage.

The other hazard of the journey was that the truck was a

216

Bedford, and Bedfords were notorious for having radiators that boiled. We had a hot following wind and, sure enough, our radiator started to boil, and we had no spare water can. Then we came across a tracked carrier vehicle abandoned six months previously, which still had water in its radiator, and we were able to replenish. There was definitely a helping hand somewhere.

Dick Cunningham served with the Royal Artillery:

Four months after being commissioned in July 1941 as a second lieutenant in the Royal Artillery I found myself in Avonmouth boarding, with some 1500 others, a ship which had been used for transporting 120 passengers and many tons of beef from Buenos Aires to Britain. Eventually we reached Suez where we were loaded on to a train which puffed gently to Cairo, and then on to lorries which took us to the Base Depot, Royal Artillery, some half-mile outside the suburb of Heliopolis. There it was proposed that I be posted to the senior regiment in the British Army, which had achieved great fame in its seven months' defence of Tobruk, 1st Regiment Royal Horse Artillery. I settled initially into "A" Battery, the Chestnut Troop. We went "up the Desert" in February 1942. In the afternoon of 3 July, my birthday, I and three fellow officers, a sergeant-major and 24 NCOs and gunners standing, under severe machine-gun fire, behind the four 25-pounder field-guns of Gardiner Troop, "E" Battery, 1st RHA took on, over open sights at a range of just over a mile, the remnants of the Afrika Korps en route, on Rommel's

217

personal orders, to capture Alexandria. We routed them, destroying 25 per cent of the attacking tanks and ourselves losing one gun and sustaining several casualties. The battle, short and small as it was, has varyingly been described as "the turning-point of the war" and as one of the war's "decisive battles". With two of the senior officers wounded and the third busy, it was left to me to describe in detail to a beaming CO the course of the battle and again and again, at his request, to the colonels, brigadiers and generals who arrived at the site.

P. E. Mott joined the Army in India, where he was working:

At last I was able to join the Army. I sold my horse, the saddle and all the tack, also my car, and put my other possessions into store. I proceeded a thousand miles south to Madras and then about 250 miles west to Bangalore, where a cadet college had been opened to train potential officers recruited in the east. I was amongst students from Kenya, Burma, Malaya and Hong Kong, as well as men from the far corners of India. We were housed in barracks converted from elephant stables, which had been divided into cubicles by wooden screens. The doors and ceilings were very high, of course.

My wife came to Bangalore and stayed in a guest house, where I was able to join her after about a month.

As cadets we were civilians and not under military law, so we had a special rate of pay, about half what I was earning in Calcutta. If we passed the course we were commissioned, if not, we went back to civvie street.

After Bangalore I went for further training at the town of Mhow in the Indian State of Indore. There was married accommodation there, and my wife was able to travel with me.

At our next stop we lived in a hotel and transport was mainly on foot, but there was quite a lot of motor transport, as all the soldiers were being taught to drive. The British gunners were equipped with 18-pounder horse-drawn guns, like those that perform these days at the Royal Tournament. The horse drivers were driving round in clapped-out Indian buses learning to drive motor vehicles, and Indian regiments were doing much the same thing. Many of the Indian recruits had come from the mountains and had not seen bullock carts, let alone cars.

My wife was expecting a baby and we decided India was not the place for her to spend the rest of the war. Going to the UK was difficult and also, of course, dangerous. I had relatives in Australia and she had friends there, so she went to Sydney. The problem of transferring money was overcome by Thomas Cook, who at that time had a banking department and could transfer funds to anywhere they had a travel shop. So we opened an account with them and my pay went into it.

Next came a dreadful journey by train crossing the Sind desert to Karachi; then by sea to Basra in Iraq. Persia, which we now call Iran, was neutral and oil-rich, but it had a leaning towards the other side, so we had a two-day war with them to secure the oil-fields. Then for me it was back across the desert to Iraq and north to the Turkish border as

Signal Officer for 11 Field Regiment (25-pounder guns). At first it was pleasant to be in green country, but when winter came we were still in shorts and shirts, living in tents. As the first flakes of snow fell, the southern Indian troops were running around like children catching the snowflakes: they had never seen snow before.

Mail came infrequently and sometimes in batches. My daughter, born in Sydney, was one month old before I knew. Letters often came in the wrong order and it became the practice to number letters so that the recipient knew if one, or indeed some, were missing. Some letters arrived bearing a stamp marked DAMAGED BY SEA WATER. They had been dried but were difficult to open and often the ink had run. For this reason many letters were written in pencil.

We had a wireless set in the Officers' Mess, but reception was very poor. However, we did hear the news of the bombing of Pearl Harbour and that the Americans were now in the war. We also heard that Rommel was pushing our troops back across the Western Desert, and it looked as though the Germans might go the whole way to Cairo. Three gunner regiments and an infantry brigade were ordered to move from Iraq to the Western Desert to try to stop them.

My regiment set off across the desert to Transjordan, as Jordan was then called, across Transjordan to Palestine, then across Sinai and over the Suez Canal and on into the Egyptian desert. The guns were designed to fire two or three miles, but almost immediately we were firing over open sights at the enemy, and the Afrika Korps were firing back at us. They seemed unstoppable, but our regiment, together with other gunners and some infantry, did stop them. We held them until new troops arrived and later the whole lot was formed into the Alamein Line.

Over the years I have heard people say "When we stood alone", but we never did stand alone, and certainly not at Alamein. There was a Greek brigade to the south and French legionnaires of the Foreign Legion, not Frenchmen in the kepi but French colonial troops wearing the fez. There were Rhodesian anti-tank gunners; there were Sotuh Africans, Indians and Australians, and no doubt others. With Germans and Italians on the other side, it was more a case of the world at war than anyone standing alone.

The moment the desert war became static we were plagued by millions of flies. They settled everywhere there was the slightest bit of damp — around our eyes, at the corners of our mouth, on any desert sores (and most of us had those). There was no way of combating them, and as a result we all had dysentery, or something akin to it. Sanitation was both basic and public, and was largely the cause of the flies.

We held the line until the Battle of Alamein, but I did have a 24-hour leave in Cairo and 12 hours in Alexandria during that time. Most of it was taken up bathing, having a hair-cut, and buying a few essentials such as desert boots, which had thick rubber soles. The leather uppers had the rough side outside and the smooth inside, and were very comfortable.

While we were at Alamein awaiting the next big move, we tried to persuade the soldiers to make out the Will forms in the back of their paybooks. Sometimes this was straightforward, but sometimes a man would say he had nothing to leave and no one to leave anything to. If I suggested he might like someone to know he had died, he might say, after much thought, "Well, there is the woman at the home." Further questions would show that he didn't know her name, the name of the home, or its correct address. I could only wonder how such men felt when others were writing and receiving mail.

Water was at a premium while we were at Alamein; petrol was more plentiful than water. Most days we washed and shaved in a mug of water and then passed on the dregs to top up the next man's mug. Clothes were not washed, but from time to time we got some new shirts and shorts.

After the Battle of Alamein, the big drive began to destroy the Italian African Empire for good. We pushed them all the way to Tunis, some 1500 miles from Egypt, most of it hard driving over awful desert. We had had to deal with some angry men on the way; now just as we thought a dip in the sea would do us good we were told to go all the way back to Egypt and prepare to invade Italy.

When we reached Alexandria, I was posted away from my British section with the gunners and took over an Indian infantry brigade HQ signal section. As India is a land of many languages, all Indian recruits to the Army were made to learn Urdu, but with the dramatic expansion during the war this educational process had gone by the board. My new unit had soldiers speaking five languages. This was overcome partly by one interpreting to another and partly by drill. However, there was one unfortunate fellow who could not talk to anyone else in the section or brigade HQ, but as there was a man in the field ambulance who knew his language we sent him there once a week for a talk!

222

The British Army has long done away with official followers. Not so the Indian Army, who retained an administrative tail of non-combatants such as cooks, laundry men, tailors, bootmakers, and so on. These non-combatants were administered and disciplined under the Indian Army Manual of Military Law. I knew this, but the application of it was new, as was the problem of men of three religions. Meat for Hindus had to be killed by Hindus and prepared in a different way from Muslim meat, and neither would eat Christian meat, i.e. bully beef. We were now in a peace situation and to meet religious requirements we received meat on hoof, live goats and sheep arriving in the ration trucks!

We had driven our vehicles hard across many miles of desert and could well have done with some replacements; instead we were stripped of our best runners and left with the unreliable ones to drive across Sinai, through Palestine and up into Lebanon to train as a mountain division, for operations along the spine of Italy. From a transport point of view this meant going over to mules. I knew a bit about horses, and mules are not that different, but I did learn two things about them. First, unlike horses, they won't drink contaminated water, so if your water is doubtful try it out on a mule. The other is they can kick sideways!

Mules cannot, of course, keep up with a motorised army, so our technique was to carry them in lorries until the roads ran out, then make them jump out and go with us into the mountains. It was more difficult getting them back in the lorries again.

We had some grim battles against the Germans in Italy, then captured the little independent state of San Marino

223

and pushed on north again. Somewhere near Forli we were pulled out of the fighting for rest and recuperation, but before we had time to experience either we were ordered to go to Salonika in Greece. We moved in American cargo ships, and mine sweepers cleared the waters of Thessalonika Bay in front of us. The local people did not know we were coming, and as we arrived the Germans moved out to the north; there was no opposition to our landing.

The Sappers worked hard building bridges and opening up the roads, and soon the Greeks were using them in the most extraordinary vehicles. There were cars with two big wheels at one end and two small ones at the other; and there were four-wheel vehicles running on three wheels, balanced by a heavy load on the appropriate corner. I even saw one vehicle with four wheels, all of different sizes.

Telegraph and telephone communications had been destroyed and the necessary wire and other stores for repair were not available. Signal officers were told to do their best. One officer, who succeeded in getting a telegraph circuit through to Veria, was asked where he got the cable; he replied "barbed wire".

VE Day was approaching and I managed to get 61 days' leave. Once back in Salonika I found that, in spite of all the soldiers' efforts, the rebuilding of Greece was going on very slowly. Relief supplies were delayed. Shortages of everything had turned the Greeks into expert thieves, and everything had to be guarded or it disappeared.

St Paul certainly left his mark on the Thessalonians, and the church had taken under their wing all the thousands of war orphans. How they fed and clothed them, goodness knows. I organised a Christmas party for one orphanage. I had a few British ranks who received a small chocolate ration and they gave up three months' ration for the party. The Indian soldiers produced most of the food. We could not provide many toys, but small things like pencils and pens were much appreciated.

VJ Day arrived unexpectedly and was followed by orders for the division to return to India. They sailed off and I stayed for a short time with the British unit who were taking over our role.

It was decided to go ahead with the partition of India, although it was obvious the Hindus and Muslims would now be scared to live side-by-side and the Muslims would be anxious to move to the safety of their new state of Pakistan. As they moved across each other's paths there was an orgy of killing, which was exacerbated by the decision to split the Army, destroying the balance of religion in each regiment. This balance had been successful since the Indian mutiny. There was now no unbiased force to police the change.

We saw the British flag pulled down and the new one hauled up. My wife and daughter were with me, and together we managed to move across India without being spattered with blood. Then there was a ghastly journey in an overcrowded boat, but at last we were home.

Ted Chaplin was captured by the Japanese in 1942:

After a two-month campaign by land down the Malayan

peninsula, the Japanese took Singapore on 15 February 1942. The artillery unit I was in was never in action, for we remained with our gun emplacements pointing seawards whilst all the action took place behind us. Like the other 85,000 Allied troops, I felt humiliated. This was the greatest defeat suffered in British military history.

The Japanese aimed to seize India by invading through Burma and sent 60,000 of their prisoners, including me, to build a 250-mile railway through the jungle connecting Siam (now Thailand) and Burma. It was constructed in a year, but we prisoners suffered: about a third died of disease, inadequate food and general maltreatment.

During this time we who were thrown together learnt how to endure and help one another. It is true that hardship brings out the best and worst in human beings. I saw plenty of the worst amongst the prisoners — leaders taking for their own benefit food issued for the general use; comrades stealing from dying men; even treachery in order to curry favour with the enemy. But I was fortunate in my companions and formed friendships with like-minded fellow prisoners that have lasted 50 years.

After the railway was built, the prisoners (what was left of us) had some respite from the gruelling construction work, and worked on maintenance. We had more leisure and in one camp I joined a group of 10 or 12 who chatted for an hour or so before dark, over mugs of burnt rice "coffee". We were mostly civilian volunteers in fighting units. Some were in jobs such as the Colonial Administrative Service or Agricultural Service; some were engineers, lawyers, architects or teachers. We lent each other books, which we discussed, and gave talks. I benefited from my association with these men, receiving intellectual stimulation I had not had in my civilian work, and had missed through my failure to go to a university.

It may surprise people that I, and most of the 60,000 prisoners, had enough leisure and opportunities to read books, but it is a fact. It helped to keep up morale and compensate for our suffering at the hands of the brutal guards, mostly Korean.

The prison life was not unrelieved gloom, and I think the experience helped younger men like me to grow up. I became a little less self-concerned and felt I could cope with whatever difficulties life might have in store. I believe it was Winston Churchill who said every man should in his youth have a period of hardship to develop strength of character. I go along with that.

The *Church of England Newspaper* (4.8.95) has given permission for the inclusion of the following personal accounts from two Japanese survivors of the atom bombs.

Masao Morihara was 18 when he entered Hiroshima as a relief worker on 6 August 1945. Since then he has suffered from various diseases, and is officially recognised as having A-bomb-induced liver dysfunction:

I think it is no exaggeration to say that my life was drastically changed by the A-bomb.

However, compared with many of those who were burned to death instantly without even uttering a word upon looking up at the lightning of the A-bomb, I feel I was lucky to have survived and was able to have my own family, even with my pains and anxiety.

In appreciation of this happiness for the past years, I have thought over and over what it means for people to live as humans and die as humans. There is nothing more precious than peace. It is the ultimate desire of human beings to abolish wars from the earth.

When the A-bomb fell on Nagasaki Sakue Shimohira was a child of 11. Her family was only 800 metres from the epicentre. Her mother and elder sister died that first day and her elder brother three days later. In 1955 her younger sister committed suicide:

I cannot and will never forget the A-bombing on Nagasaki on 9 August 1945. In a flash of light I was blown and toppled in an air-raid shelter located about 1 km from what would become the hypocentre. With a voice saying, "Is there anyone from Kamaba Town Group Number 8?" I came to my senses. Some moments before there were many people taking refuge in the shelter, but when the All Clear sounded, many boys delightedly rushed out and they disappeared. Only one-third of those who had taken refuge together remained inside.

Outside, I saw many people wandering about whose sex could not be distinguished. Their eyeballs were protruding, intestines out from their bowels and their hair gone. A young man whose face swelled like a pumpkin and was seriously burned was crying loudly. A mother was holding her baby which was burned black. She herself was severely burned but still tried to survive. There were charred corpses scattered here and there.

The town, which had been an ordinary residential area just a moment before, burned into total debris in an instant. I tried to look for my house but everything in the area was totally destroyed and there was no clue.

I was at a loss, not knowing how to find my family. It was in the evening when my father finally came and found me. The scenes of parents and children calling each other and holding each other with the delight of confirming each other's survival are still printed on my mind.

I saw the skin of people peeling off when touched with hands, just like the peel of tomatoes. People frantically cried for water saying, "Give me water, give me water". They ran, walked and crawled to the Urakami River through flaring fires and at last reached the riverbank and drank water, only to breathe their last. The surface of the river was covered with corpses. Corpses were flowing away, some of them stuck on rocks, others piling over them — the scene was the very hell on earth.

After much effort we finally found our house. A man living next to us was charred to death, in a figure of looking up to the sky, with his arms folded.

My mother, in a figure of sitting, was also so charred that I could not identify the body as my mother. Her body looked so fragile that it would have crumbled down into pieces if I had hugged her, crying "Mom".

My sister also died, leaving an 18-month-old baby behind. My brother kept crying, "I don't want to die. I don't want to die", and vomiting something yellow. On the third day he breathed his last.

Jim West served in the Indian Army:

Towards the end of 1943 the 14th Indian Division, to which we were attached, was withdrawn from Burma to form a training division to teach new recruits the elementary techniques required for survival in the jungle. As the war progressed, more and more Indians were being commissioned into the Indian Army, a very different situation from pre-war days when the Army was staffed predominantly with officers drawn from Britain. We were one of the first battalions to have an Indian Commanding Officer, a very fine Sikh officer, with whom I enjoyed a good relationship, serving as his adjutant. My fellow Indian officers were well educated, intelligent and capable; we became good friends with them and held them in high regard. I could readily understand the Indians' desire for independence, and it seemed right that the British should hand the government over to them as soon as the war was over.

At the general election after VE Day in 1945, members of the Armed Forces serving overseas were given a postal vote. I decided that I would give my first ever vote to whichever party offered India unqualified independence. As this was promised unequivocally by Labour, but only with qualifications by the Conservatives, Clement Attlee got my vote. The majority of the Services' vote was said to have been pro-Labour in 1945. I do not think this was a vote against Winston Churchill himself; rather it was a vote against the old Conservative regime of the 1930s, which was held responsible for depression and unemployment at home and the appeasement of dictators abroad.

In July 1945, I was given a month's leave to return to England. I flew home from Karachi in a Dakota with a few other lucky leave-takers. We spent one night at Tel Aviv and another in Sicily, then flew direct to England, landing at an airfield in the heart of Somerset on a glorious summer day. It was a wonderful way to arrive home, and England had never looked greener or more beautiful. We spent our first evening drinking draught cider and playing skittles in the local pub.

While I was on leave the atom bombs were dropped on Hiroshima and Nagasaki, and the war with Japan ended. I immediately contacted the India Office and to my surprise and delight was granted immediate release from the Army.

Keith Spooner was not a natural soldier but, like many others, learnt to submit to the rigours of military discipline:

The Battle of Britain came as an early and welcome release from the tedium and contrived tantrums of parade-ground soldiering. I was by this time a rifle platoon runner for the 1st London Scottish Battalion, in charge of a cast-iron War Department bicycle, complete with paraffin lamp, for which I had to draw a supply of matches from the quarterbloke's store. We had a platoon sergeant-major, a rank that was shortly to be discontinued, in lieu of an officer, and this man, a bandy-legged swashbuckler known as "Sailor" because he had at one time commanded some sort of a ship, treated me with a mocking and not unaffectionate exasperation, which somehow gained my acceptance and made me feel more at home in the Army than I would ever have thought possible.

The Battle of Britain was fought largely over our heads as we daily dug defences behind the Kent coast and stood-to-arms at every dawn and dusk, giving us a stimulating sense of manning a threatened nation's ramparts. Those extraordinary months did much to ameliorate the "diabolical liberties" the Army took upon us, to make us feel that we were no longer merely playing at soldiers. It was a golden summer, too, of almost unbroken fine weather, with a fighter's sun by day, a bomber's moon at night, warming the seeds of comradeship that would fructify so fully later.

We were frequently exhausted after eight hours of digging, the stand-tos, the guards and pickets, rarely managing more than a few consecutive hours of sleep; yet we grumbled less, obeyed orders without reck or resentment, applied ourselves to *practical* soldiering, and in a languor of fatigue were touched by all nature's beautiful, yet homely, constituents, savouring the smallest comforts and bodily dispensations. I know that despite the Army's absolute autonomy, the demands and the uncertain future, my whole response to life deepened permanently during that year.

In 1941, disaffection set in seriously. Hitler had invaded Russia, not Britain, and Army life promised only an eternal recurrence of guards, cookhouse fatigues, repetitive training and, above all, gruelling and shambolical "schemes", as field exercises lasting for days and nights on end were called.

By this time, however, as the Army is adept at finding square holes for its square pegs, I had been posted with other misfits and rebels to the Signals, a platoon noted for its unorthodoxy, and where other than purely parade-ground and weaponry virtues prevailed. I had found my Army niche.

Eventually, in July 1943 and three and a half years since most of us had joined the Army, we were baptised by fire on Catania Plain in Sicily, the service conducted by the Spandaus, six-inch mortars, *Nebelwerfers* (multi-barrelled dittos) and 88-millimetre guns of the Hermann Goering and 1st German Parachute Divisions.

This fiery initiation was the prelude to nearly two years of intermittent exposure to the "sharp-end", during which time we amply experienced what Fred Majdalany has described as "the definitive horror of war and the curiously perverse paradoxical nobility of battle".

When, early in May 1945, all German forces south of the Alps surrendered, we had reached the small town of Dolo, a few miles inland from Venice, and there were very few original faces left in the battalion to celebrate the event. I, for one, could hardly believe my astonishing good fortune; I had plodded through it all, innumerable bullets and shell fragments somehow missing such a gangling target, my attenuated frame apparently impervious to the prevalent diseases.

Much of the experience has come to seem in retrospect increasingly unreal. Was it really a youthful forerunner of

233

today's sedentary pensioner who shambled through the rigours of training and into battle itself, dourly, reluctantly, often in apprehensive dread, sometimes in sheerest terror? It rather seems that I am contemplating the vicissitudes — comical, lamentable and stark — of another person altogether, and it's not possible now to enter truly into his reactions, his responses. The extremes of fear, fatigue and stress can no more be invoked by memory than the unique stench of death's decay by the olfactory sense. And can I really explain the ambivalence of my feelings towards war experience now, even the basic satisfaction — pride — that it was undergone?

Dennis Thompson joined the King's Royal Rifle Corps in May 1941:

By September I was en route for the Middle East. To avoid the German submarines we sailed far out into the North Atlantic, turning south some 300 miles from Iceland until we were opposite Freetown, Sierra Leone, our first port of call. From there our route was down the west coast of Africa, round the Cape of Good Hope, and into Durban, where we, like all other troops, were made very welcome by the South Africans. It made a pleasant change from the cramped conditions on the troopship and was much appreciated.

From Durban we sailed to Aden and thence up the Red Sea and Gulf of Suez to Port Taufiq at the southern end of the Suez Canal.

234

Our convoy was very fortunate, with no losses, and, having sailed 20,000 miles in her, we had become quite attached to the SS *Franconia*. Her captain on that voyage was James Bisset, who later took over the *Queen Mary* on her many unescorted dashes across the Atlantic. After disembarking we went by train to a holding camp under canvas outside Cairo, within sight of the Pyramids.

On the first day of January 1942 I was in action for the first time in the Western Desert. The previous November the British Army had started a new offensive against Rommel, after the Germans had reinforced the retreating Italians. For ten months with the 7th Armoured Brigade (Desert Rats) we fluctuated between "the wire", as it was called (the boundary between Egypt and Cyrenaica), and El Agheila in Libya. The sudden advances and strategic withdrawals were commonly known to the troops as "the Gazala gallop".

I missed the Battle of Alamein, as due to dysentery, jaundice and tonsillitis I had spells in hospital, followed by convalescence. Then I went to Palestine, being posted to the newly formed Middle East School of Infantry, where officers received their final training for war, with the possibility of a land war in Japan. Palestine and the hill area where training took place was by all accounts similar to Japan. Our base was at Acre, 12 miles north of Haifa.

I returned to England five months after the war in Europe ended. I was then in the company office of a training battalion in Wiltshire — quite a change from war conditions, but it was August 1946 before I was demobbed.

Audrey Dench became a radio mechanic in the WRNS:

I was 18 when I joined the WRNS in 1943. They were looking for more technical people and, because I had matriculated, I was ear-marked for the technical side. We started with seven days' training at the old Cancer Research Station in Mill Hill. My first posting was to Battersea to train as a radio mechanic. This was fine by me, as my family lived in Wandsworth and we were billeted in Crosby Hall, by Battersea Bridge. We had four and a half months training in general electrical theory at either Battersea or Chelsea Polytechnic. Each morning I marched past Battersea Park en route for Battersea Polytechnic with the others for a day of lectures on electrical theory, and work in electrical and mechanical workshops where we did soldering, filed metal, and learnt how to splice wires and ropes. Our living quarters had been a hostel for overseas students before the war and were very good, as was the food.

At the end of that time, we were despatched to a camp called HMS Ariel near Warrington, close to a village named Culcheth. It was in November, when Lancashire was particularly drab and drear. We spent our days studying radio sets and learning about special circuits and many other things which mean little to me now. We also had to do squad drill, trained by a naval gunnery instructor. Ours could never get over having to drill us girls, who regularly got the giggles from his commands. "Wipe it orff" was one of his favourite expressions. All this came to a conclusion when we passed (or failed) our exams and were posted all over the country. I'm sure that most of us did not know too much after that crammed course but off we went to do our best for King and Country.

My posting was to Donibristle, close to the Forth and near Rosyth. It had a splendid view looking down over the Forth Bridge, which was some distance away, and across to Edinburgh. We worked on what seemed terrible old aircraft which the Fleet Air Arm had to use, but the pilots did wonders in them. We Wrens lived in a big house some distance from the aerodrome but we had regular transport to and fro. We had to service radio equipment on aircraft and test it ready for use. The equipment we used was large and heavy, and the young "jolly Jacks" often took pity on us and helped us with the heavy work. I was small and rather blonde, and even the big girls on our section insisted on carrying heavy things for me!

After a while, some of us were asked if we would like to fly in the aircraft to test the equipment. I couldn't wait to get the chance and, though I know it was hazardous, I loved it. When you are 19 you don't think too much about whether you will get down safely. You feel that you are immortal. The pilot would take the aircraft up and test the engine in various ways. This always included finding the stalling speed by throttling back the engine until it cut out and you dived from the sky. The test, as far as I was concerned, was whether they would get the engine to start up again but, luckily for me, it always did when I went up. We also used to fly along the Forth over Edinburgh and Stirling and we would go air-firing the guns on targets in the River Forth.

There was never enough flying for me, and when I was demobbed, I found family life in London very stifling.

Elizabeth Hughes joined the WRNS:

When we WRNS trainees arrived at Mill Hill in London we were issued with three scratchy woollen vests, four pairs of thick woollen stockings, suspender belt, calico bra and even a toothbrush and shoe brushes, which I still use. The quality of the uniform, warm and thick, was very good. I suppose they knew we would be in huts and on watch in cold, draughty places. The only impractical issue was the starched white collar that had to be changed daily. The studs dug into our necks back and front. I managed to use my father's smaller ones. The plain white shirts were very good cotton. After we were demobilised I dyed mine bright colours and used them for years.

Eventually I was sent to Plymouth to become a Royal Marine Wren. So off came the HMS band on my hat; instead a red flash was sewn on and the Globe and Laurel badge. We were based in Stonehouse Barracks where I found that other Wrens did not have the daily drilling and marching we suffered. An old Colour Sergeant would shout out remarks such as "Open your legs; you won't drop anything", or "You're having it easy. My old woman has seven children and knows what hard work is." This was very amusing for the men who usually crammed the barrack windows. When it was my turn to be marker Wren the sergeant would so engineer it that I marched out to stand in a puddle (the whole parade ground was pitted with bomb craters). He would then say, "Don't wet yourself."

Once we were detailed to help a squad of sailors assisting at a local gymkhana to raise money for "Wings for Victory" week. Whilst there they kept drinking the local scrumpy, thinking it was harmless. By packing-up time they were mostly legless and we Wrens lifted them up into our truck. I'd been in the middle of an art teacher's diploma before joining up, so I entered for a county poster competition for "Wings for Victory" and won, much to my surprise.

We slept in the few remaining unbombed houses two miles away. There we had to "swab the decks and walls"; it must have ruined the house and it always seemed damp. I hated sleeping on the third bunk up as the electric bulb was just a foot away from my head. Those getting up to prepare for night watch switched it on regardless.

Crossing Plymouth, which was just rubble, never worried me. Because there were patrolling Military Police there was rarely any trouble, only the odd bottle whizzing by. On the rare home leaves we saved up for days to make it worthwhile. I think I had only two home visits to Wales.

Some weeks we were taken by lorry to Thurlestone Commando training camp to work in draughty old huts. Little did I know that my future husband was on a course training for the Arnhem drop! He had been so pleased to miss a Far East draft, having just returned from the invasion of Sicily.

As demob grew nearer, we were very busy preparing the Marine documents for the men. Many were the sad letters from families. On VJ Day we all marched down to The Hoe. The marching was a shambles, but who cared? There was a local band at the end of the column and the RN band in front; neither kept to the same tempo. I and others were dressed oddly: I had pyjamas under my bell-bottoms.

This day it was drizzling heavily on The Hoe, as it often was. I always had trouble with my hair as it was so strong and bushy and we had to keep it off the collar.

Mervyn Mott was working as a Civil Servant in London at the outbreak of war, and as he was in a reserved occupation he was not liable to call up until 1942. After active service in the RNVR, he ended his naval career in Harrods Furniture Repository's basement:

By 1942 the Government had moved the goal-posts as far as reserved occupations were concerned; I was called for a medical examination and passed "A1" fit for active service. I volunteered for the Royal Navy and on 4 March 1942 (just after my 27th birthday), I said goodbye to my wife and two young children and journeyed by rail to Plymouth, travelling on a free pass to commence my training.

At the end of ten weeks' basic training we were sorted according to our aptitudes and spent a further two weeks doing more specialised training in another camp. This was followed by a few days' leave and then I was drafted to HMS *Albrighton*, a Hunt-class destroyer of First Destroyer Flotilla based at Portsmouth. Most of the time we were engaged on protective coastal convoy duty, through the English Channel, but we occasionally took part in offensive patrols against enemy shipping

One day while we were in port, I was sent ashore to be

interviewed by a board as possible officer material, and was accepted, but returned to my ship to gain more sea experience.

In August 1942, we took part in some exercises off the Dorset coast, which turned out to be a practice for the Dieppe raid, although we were not aware of this until we sailed for the French coast. A few days later, during the raid itself (which served to confuse the enemy about our future strategy), the ship was hit by at least three shells. We suffered casualties and extensive damage, but were able to pick up survivors from our sister ship HMS *Berkeley*, which was badly damaged. I spent most of the action in the transmitting station, but then I was sent out on deck to help pick up survivors and saw the launch of the torpedo which we used to sink HMS *Berkeley* after her crew had been removed.

On return to Portsmouth we had to land the survivors and then land all our remaining ammunition before we could dock the ship. It was then that I learned that a shell had passed right through the ship without exploding, a few feet below where I had been sitting. The following day I was sent on leave to await a place at HMS King Alfred (the officer training base). We spent three months in intensive training there, completed by an examination, which I passed. I was promoted to the rank of Temporary Sub-Lieutenant RNVR on 20 November 1942 and, after another two weeks spent on a navigation course and a few days leave, on 29 December 1942 I joined HMS *Manxmaid*, which was undergoing a refit at Leith docks. She was an old cross-Channel ferry and was still able to speed at 16 knots. For the next 11 months we acted as a target ship for Fleet Air Arm practice, mainly in the Firth of Forth.

In November 1943 I was promoted to Temporary Lieutenant RNVR. There was an influenza epidemic on board and as we carried no medical officer I had to help look after the patients. Then I became ill myself and was taken ashore with pneumonia. Eventually I was sent home by train from Edinburgh to London in the depth of winter and by the time I reached home I had a relapse and needed a further spell in bed.

When I recovered I was appointed to HMS *Turtle*, a large shore camp near Poole, as acting First Lieutenant and remained there over the D-Day period. The camp housed 2000 naval and Royal Marine personnel and a further 2000 US Navy sailors and US coastguards. The whole area was surrounded by a barbed-wire fence and patrolled by armed sentries. Every night a motor boat toured Poole harbour dropping depth charges to discourage infiltration by enemy divers. Swimming was not a popular sport!

Shortly before D-Day, the Captain ordered a full parade of all personnel and took the salute. It was my privilege to lead this parade. A few days later most of the marchers left us for the D-Day landings in 212 craft of various types, and HMS *Turtle* was left comparatively deserted, although we continued to serve as a supply base for the Forces in Europe for some months.

After serving in the Mediterranean I was found unfit for sea service and recommended for home and harbour duties. My last appointment was as Tools Officer and assistant to the Lieutenant Commander in charge of 500 shipwrights (all awaiting demobilisation), who were carrying out bomb damage repairs in the Brixton area of London. Our barracks was the basement of Harrods Furniture Repository and we had our own three-ton lorry fleet to convey us and the equipment to our work area.

If a ceiling collapsed it was extraordinary how many tools the ratings "lost" in the rubble. It was a different matter when over a hundred scaffold boards disappeared. A local builder who was also working in the area did not realise that, in truc Navy fashion, they were stamped and therefore identifiable.

Eventually my own date of demobilisation arrived and, on 4 April 1946, I passed through the demobilisation centre near Crystal Palace and was issued with a "demob suit" and accessories, so that I could make my way home as a civilian and recommence my career as a Civil Servant.

Ernie Knight enlisted in the Royal Navy at Chatham on 1 March 1941, when he was only 16. Walter Edmonds also joined the Navy in 1941 when he, too, was 16, but he enlisted at Devonport. From 1943 to 1945 they were firm friends:

After basic training at Chatham I was sent in November 1941 to join HMS *Gambia*, a new cruiser. Whilst we were at Scapa Flow early in 1942 working up gunnery and other trials, it was decided that HMS *Gambia* and HMS *Frobisher* would sail with a convoy from Greenock to the Far East to join the 4th Cruiser Squadron.

In February 1942 I had three days' leave. When I left

my home at Canterbury and reached the end of the road, I looked back. My mother was still standing at the gate, waving to me. I was never to see her again, as she died in August 1944 whilst I was in the Far East.

My action station was the cordite handling room, under the shell room literally at the bottom of the ship, with watertight hatches battened down and locked. It was impossible to open them from the inside. What a thought! But my youth maybe did away with any fear. I felt fate had been kind to me, especially as others who were at school with me were killed aged only 16.

In 1943 when it was decided to make HMS *Gambia* a New Zealand ship, HMNZ *Gambia*, several of us were drafted around the Fleet and I went to the Submarine Depot ship, HMS *Adamant*. There I met Walter Edmonds for the first time. We were mates for two and a half years until 1945.

Walter had been sent to HMS *Adamant* at Greenock early in 1942 when she was about to sail to the Far East. While we were at Mombasa Fleet anchorage in 1943 both of us on HMS *Adamant*, we went ashore on leave from 1 p.m. to 10 p.m. After a walk through the town we decided to go to the Fleet canteen for a couple of drinks. The Fleet canteen was in Salam Road, off Kilidini Road, so after we had had quite a few beers I decided that the walk up Salam Road and then down Kilidini Road to the jetties at the docks was too long. To save time and energy (it was a typical black African night) we would take a short cut through the shrub and jungle, which would save approximately a mile.

We had gone about 500 yards when I stood on

THE ARMED FORCES AND THEIR IMPACT

something soft and slippery: it coiled over my foot. Walter agrees with me that Roger Bannister was not the first man to do the mile in four minutes!

We left *Adamant* together and joined the *Valiant*, as she was on her way back to England. I last saw Walter at Plymouth in February 1945. As I was a Chatham rating I went back to Chatham. I eventually left the Royal Navy in November 1948. Walter also left the Navy in 1948. It was a great joy to be reunited with him in 1995.

Arnold Mott joined the RAF Volunteer Reserve in 1938, while employed in a bank, and commenced training as a pilot at Redhill aerodrome in June 1939. He had some hair-raising experiences during the war:

I was called up for full-time service with the Royal Air Force at the outbreak of war and was posted to Cambridge for basic training, followed by further flying training at Cambridge aerodrome. In April 1940 I transferred to Shawbury, in Shropshire, to learn to fly twin-engined aircraft, during which time I had my first experience of war. A German intruder aircraft dropped a stick of bombs across the barracks, one of which landed outside my bedroom window, covering me with glass.

In October I was posted to 78 (Heavy Bomber) Squadron at Dishforth, Yorkshire, flying Whitleys for bombing operations. I flew on 19 bombing missions against targets varying between the French and Belgian Channel ports, and two attacks over Berlin.

After spending Christmas in England I took the standby aircraft on a raid against the submarine base at Lorient, Brittany. Although I experienced a minor engine problem while still over England, I decided that, as we were only on a short trip, we would continue to the target as ordered. We met heavy anti-aircraft defences over the target area and shortly after dropping our bombs suffered a near miss from a large shell, which set one engine on fire.

Unfortunately I was unable to maintain level height with only one engine and the other one still on fire, so I ordered the crew to take to their parachutes. When the last one had gone, I jumped through the escape hatch and, seconds later, landed in a churchyard compost heap just as the aircraft crashed in flames a couple of fields away. Within a few minutes, I was picked up by a Frenchman who took me to his home, gave me a hot drink and then hurried me to the outskirts of his village indicating that I should hurry away, because a German patrol was in the vicinity.

Three days later, after failing to find a boat to cross the Channel, I made contact with Resistance workers, who provided me with civilian clothes. I stayed with them for six months, improving my French and assisting them to identify and transmit to England details of German troop movements and other useful information.

My stay with those people ended suddenly when one of my crew, who was sheltering in the same town, was arrested by the Germans and taken to their barracks for interrogation. As he knew I was living near, I decided to leave immediately and caught the first train away from the town. I left the train at a small station in the country and headed south on foot, towards the Demarcation Line near

Poitiers and then to the Pyrenees, which I crossed near Latour-de-Carol and continued, over the Spanish frontier, south towards Barcelona.

After my long walk, in shoes a size too small, with my feet reduced to two big blisters, I found it difficult to walk into the British Consulate without limping. I was offered a drink and opted for a cup of strong tea, which convinced them that I really was British.

The Consul arranged for me to be billeted with his chauffeur in Barcelona, where the chauffeur's wife tended my feet and looked after me for a couple of weeks before returning me to the Consulate, from where I was taken by official car to the Embassy at Madrid.

I stayed at the Embassy with two or three other escaped airmen for several days until tickets had been obtained for us to travel by train from Madrid to La Linea, thence to Gibraltar. I returned to England on an Australian Sunderland Flying Boat, the captain of which befriended me at Gibraltar and agreed to my flying with him and his crew as "supernumary crew", instead of waiting for the next troopship.

My parents were surprised and delighted to see me, having had no news of me since the official telegram about a year earlier saying that I had failed to return from an operation sortie and, later, that I was presumed dead! After a week at home, I reported to the Air Ministry for debriefing and was then posted to No. 138 (Special Duties) Squadron, whose main task was to deliver agents by parachute into enemy-occupied territories and later collect them by Lysander Aircraft, landing at night on remote fields in France.

I was transferred to 161 Squadron, a new squadron formed specifically to do the night recovery jobs, after a short stay on 138 Squadron. At the end of May 1942 my reception committee in France had to change the landing field at short notice, because of troop manoeuvres, and could not warn me. However, as the new field was only a couple of miles from the original one, they flashed my "Clear to land" code. Unfortunately, they had failed to see that half of the field had been ploughed up during the afternoon and my aeroplane got bogged down when I landed.

As I was unable to move the aircraft, I had to leave it and disappear quickly into the country. The leader of my reception committee told me that, if I walked across country for about a mile till I reached a small road, and followed that to a village, I would find a bicycle leaning against the Post Office wall. I took it and set off south, although it was well after curfew. About half an hour later I went into a field and hid under the hedge until I heard other people on the road soon after daylight, then I rode on again until, at about midday, I had a puncture.

There was no tool bag or repair kit on the machine, so I sat at the roadside and, with difficulty, forced off the wheel cover, then tied a knot in the inner tube where I found the puncture, and tried to refit the cover. At that moment a policeman arrived in a small car; he asked for my bicycle permit and identity papers. In the absence of these he arrested me and drove me to the barracks at Chateauroux.

After several days under interrogation there, I was escorted to a French POW camp north of Nice, where I found about a hundred British prisoners from all services, including about a dozen officers.

A few months later we were transferred to the prison at Lyons for a few days before going to a converted army camp near Grenoble. There the French commandant called me to his office and said that, if the Italians or Germans took over control of the camp, I should be careful. He then showed me a dossier of my exploits during my stay in France in 1941, which could cause me some embarrassment if I was caught by the Germans.

Shortly afterwards, the Italian troops took over guard duties at our camp and, within a few days, moved us all by bus to Gavi concentration camp, an old castle to the north of Genoa. Several days before the Italian armistice with the Allied Forces, Gavi camp was taken over by German troops and within days we were moved to a collection point at a nearby sports stadium, where we found about a thousand other POWs staying in the open with only a blanket or a greatcoat for shelter. Then we were herded into a train to be taken to German POW camps in Austria.

Bearing in mind the warning I had received from the French commandant, I decided not to wait until we reached Austria so, with the help of others in my cattle truck, I jumped from the train, receiving only minor injuries, and made my way to the foothills of the Alps. There I met Micky, an RAF officer, who had been with me in the prison camp, and some partisans, who helped us along towards Yugoslavia. When we reached Slovenia we were confronted by a couple of men with machine-guns, who spoke no English, French or Italian, and assumed we were Germans because of the similarity of our language to German.

After some interrogation at the headquarters of the band,

we were given a spade each and made to dig our own graves but, during the lunch break, the local British liaison officer, whom I had known in the French camp many months earlier, arrived. He recognised me and obtained our release.

Later we made our way back into Italy and south across the river Po towards Venice and Rimini, spending the nights at farms. We managed to acquire a boat, having met five other POWs who wanted to go with us.

After three days and nights at sea, most of the crew were very seasick and insisted that we make for land as soon as possible, so we turned westwards towards the land we could see on the horizon. This we reached, to be confronted by a detachment of Gurkhas of the 5th Indian Division.

During interrogation by the Gurkha officer I mentioned that my younger brother was serving in the 5th Indian Division. The officer telephoned to his Brigade Headquarters with the result that my brother came into the tent, having just returned from Monte Cassino with a slight face wound.

On arrival at the ex-POW collection unit at Naples, I was called to Cairo for attachment to No. 1 Special Force at Bari in Italy to assist in the delivery of supplies by air to the partisans in Yugoslavia.

After two months at Bari, I was repatriated to England and posted to No. 1 Ferry Unit, to collect new aircraft from the factories and fly them to destinations in Europe, West Africa and Egypt, as replacements for war-damaged aircraft.

I continued ferrying aircraft until September 1947, when

I was sent to Titchfield Reserve Centre, as Chief Instructor, until June 1950, after which I was posted to a Staff appointment at Headquarters Home Command.

Joan Newall served in the WAAF as a meteorologist:

In May 1942 I volunteered to join the WAAF and I was accepted to train as a meteorologist. I had to report to Innsworth, Gloucester, and was fortunate to spend only a week squarebashing, as I was then sent to London to begin the training course in place of a Waaf who was ill. We learnt about the indoor and outdoor recording instruments used; the formation of clouds; how to code the weather for reports and how to plot the charts from reports around the country. Among other things we learnt how to recognise "fronts" and how to track pilot balloons.

I was posted to Porton, the Chemical Defence Experimental Station, near Salisbury, where Waafs were taking over the duties of young men in the Met Office who were being called up. We were on detachment from Old Sarum RAF Station, who paid us.

Porton camp was staffed by Royal Artillery and ATS, and the Waafs came under the jurisdiction of the ATS Officer in charge. We had a WAAf Officer in the Met Office who was one of the forecasters of the local weather. Our duties were: plotting the charts with weather reports received from other stations by teleprinter (we did not send out our reports); and taking observations, especially when experiments were being carried out. Sometimes this meant going away from camp: for instance, when smoke screens were being tested in a town I might have to measure wind, and wet and dry temperatures in a field in the middle of the night; or sit on shore taking similar observations while a boat made smoke screens up and down a channel.

In 1943 the WAAf Officer and I spent about six weeks in Scotland, at the time that Gruinard Island was contaminated with anthrax. She forecast the weather from the charts which I plotted from weather reports taken down from wireless reports and decoded each day. As we were the only females in the party we lived in a beach house and I (a LACW — Leading Aircraft Woman) ate in the officers' mess, with the officers and boffins. It was not unusual to meet Highland cattle when we went to the beach house in the evenings.

Eventually there were 11 Waafs at the Met Office at Porton. Besides carrying out the usual duties, each of us was "attached" to one of the specialist men in the office. My "chief" studied wind. He had anemometers set at different heights and recorded their revolutions (and therefore the wind force) every 15 minutes. Subsequently I was required to do calculations, aided by a slide rule, and then draw graphs. Another job I did was to calibrate anemometers in the wind tunnel and also do experiments using "bad egg" gas. This meant I had to rush to open the doors to let out the revolting smell after each experiment.

With 11 Waafs in the Met Office, someone decided that we should have some corporals (we were all LACWs), and three of us had to go to Wilmslow on an NCO course for corporals, early in 1944. Later that year, in October, I was surprised to be made sergeant. It did not make a lot of difference to life, only added a few responsibilities. We had, of course, been doing NCO duty and I remember being on duty on the night of 5-6 June 1944 when the second front began and planes went over all through the night.

I was married in June 1945 to someone I had met before the war, and was discharged from the WAAF at the beginning of August 1945, almost exactly three years after I had arrived at Porton.

CHAPTER
ELEVEN

Scouts, Guides, Clubs

Children who had joined Boy Scouts, Girl Guides or the Boys' Brigade were able to help the war effort in many ways. Boys aged 14 and over could also become members of the Junior Training Corps (formerly the Officers' Training Corps), the Air Training Corps or the Sea Cadet Force. There were similar organisations for girls.

However, it was the well-established Scouts and Guides that had the greatest number of members, and their motto of "Be prepared" and commitment to help others made them particularly useful during the war. Some of the troops and companies in urban districts lost not only leaders who were called up but also many of their members as they were evacuated. But their loss was to be the gain of many country areas that had only small groups of Scouts and Guides, or none at all. Soon new troops and companies were flourishing, squeezing into any available accommodation, often meeting during the daytime on Saturdays to avoid raids and black-out.

Many did voluntary work in hospitals, helping

prepare the supper trolleys for the patients, doing the washing-up and helping in the kitchen. Even Cubs and Brownies helped the older boys and girls with the many collections needed to aid the war effort — waste paper, jam jars, scrap iron and in the autumn rose hips, acorns and conkers.

Much of the leadership now fell on women, who at times acted as Scout Mistresses. Organising summer camps was an added problem — finding a suitable site and then providing food. If the camp lasted a week or more, the campers took their ration books so that the Scout or Guide acting as quartermaster could get a bulk supply permit from the local Food Office. For shorter periods each camper had to contribute an appropriate fraction of his/her ration for the week; these were then pooled and the QM had to use them to improvise meals as best he or she could.

With all clothing on ration, providing uniforms for new recruits and those who were outgrowing their current ones was another problem, many making do with second-hand clothes and equipment.

VE Day did not mean the end of the problem, as for a while conditions became worse rather than better, but at least there was no more bombing or black-out, and it was possible to gather round the camp-fire at night again.

In 1946 the Scout Jamboree was celebrated in Plymouth, with the new Chief Scout, Lord Rowallan, addressing the troops. He paid tribute to the magnificent work the Plymouth Scouts had done in the blitz (as had the Guides), and to the bravery shown by individual members.

Henry Patterson gained much from Scouts, and gave much back. Glasgow was the home of the Boys' Brigade and there was friendly rivalry between the two movements:

I was born in 1933, the year Hitler came to power, and what an influence he has been on my life! He stole much of my childhood: we had to grow up and be too responsible too soon.

In 1944 I joined the local Scout troop, the 152 Boy Scouts. I was over 11 and had just moved to the senior secondary school, having passed what was then called the qualifying examination. I knew most of the boys in the troop from school or Sunday school and I stayed with that troop for a long time, going through all the ranks from Scout in the Springbok Patrol, Seconder in the Tigers, to Patrol Leader (PL) in the Buffaloes. Eventually I became Troop Leader and then Assistant Scout Master (ASM). I left when I was about 20 with my warrant returned with thanks from Lord Rowallan, the Chief Scout. Leaving was really due to the pressure of time, my studies as an undergraduate, playing rugby and discovering that girls could be interesting.

By the time I left, nearly half of my life had been in the Scouts. The 152 was a large troop with about a hundred boys in the troop and 50 in the Cub Scouts. I never was a Cub because of wartime evacuation. The troop continued with gradually decreasing numbers for at least another 15 years.

Obtaining the uniform was a struggle for my mother, but we visited the Scout Shop, where valuable clothing coupons were surrendered, along with even more valuable money. We purchased a dark blue, heavy shirt, a red and blue triangular neckerchief and a woggle to keep the neckerchief in place. Second-hand I got the leather belt with the Scouts' fleur-de-lys badge as a buckle, and the big Boer War hat which, despite much ironing, never attained a flat, straight brim. My troop wore kilts, and this was no problem as I had always had a kilt and often wore it to school. Kilts lasted a lot longer than trousers because of the extra material and because they could be worn from below the knees until they became miniskirts.

Over the right shirt pocket was sewn a yellow badge with the City of Glasgow's ancient arms on it and on the left shoulder the legend "152 Boy Scouts (Glasgow)". The first task of the recruit was to learn the Scout promise and laws off by heart: "On my honour I promise to do my best, to do my duty to God and the King, to help other people at all times and to obey the Scout Law." This, plus a few other simple tasks, earned the Tenderfoot badge and I became a real Scout.

Our regular Friday evening meetings began at 7.30 p.m. in the gym of the primary school I had attended. The Scout Leader, Andy Couper, seemed very, very old, but we respected him immensely. There were two ASMs who must have been unfit for war service. Every evening started with a parade and an inspection for cleanliness and correct uniform. Shoes had to be polished. We formed up in patrols with the PL at the front and the Seconder at the rear, to watch our behaviour. After intimations, we spent about 15 minutes learning to come to attention, march, halt, about turn, etc. Quite easy except for the chap who could march only with his right arm going forward with his right foot.

We broke off then into our patrol corners to work for badges and so on. Second Class and First Class badges involved about ten separate items each to be learned and examined plus some nights camping. I think ten nights camping for Second Class and 20 for First Class, but not necessarily all in one expedition. We learnt about First Aid, knots and lashings, signalling, names of common trees and birds, etc. I loved the knots and lashings and can still do them all.

The First Class badge was completed with a journey that involved map-reading, map-making and camping out in the middle of a 20-mile hike. We had learned already about grid reference numbers and how to use a compass. I was given the two largest Scouts to accompany me, but I was the leader and wrote the report. It felt good to be a Scout (First Class). I never became a King's Scout, which was the next step. In addition, there were proficiency badges. These badges were sewn on the sleeves, and promotion white stripes were sewn on the pocket. Some people could have done with longer sleeves. Incidentally, the shirts were short-sleeved, which could be jolly cold at church parades.

My very first camp was only two nights, a long weekend, and we had to put up our tent, light the wood fire and cook for ourselves. The ancient bell tent had a bit sawn off the pole, so we had to put a slice of log under it and hold it in place while the guy ropes were attached to the pegs. "Remember to slacken the ropes at night in case they shrink and tear the canvas." Modern tents are so much better. I returned home utterly exhausted as I had hardly slept while away. I did a lot of camping and became better at it.

A few of us used to call for a boy called Kenny on our way to the Scouts. He was confined to a wheelchair but he sure was enthusiastic about coming with us. We went out collecting for various charities from time to time, including the Earl Haig Fund.

Our Friday evening meetings ended at 9 p.m. with another parade and the singing of the first verses of "Abide with Me" (our SM's favourite hymn) and the National Anthem. I am sure that we took the words of the hymn literally rather than metaphorically. Later on I played the piano for this, as I had been having music lessons. I copied the scores out and kept them in my Scout shirt pocket.

We attended church parades about six times each year. Our objective was to be better turned out and march more smartly than the Boys' Brigade Company based at the church and, of course, better than the Girl Guides. We carried our colours into church taking care not to spear the point of the flag on the balcony of the church — a painful experience. The BB were very good too with their pipe band. Some Scout troops had a band but we did not manage one. We had a poor opinion of BB camping as they seemed to camp in huts or with camp beds, and took adults along to cook for them. All the Scouts in Glasgow, along with other uniformed youth organisations, took part in a march-past after VE Day, doing our "eyes right" in George Square before the Lord Provost and other dignitaries standing at the Cenotaph. We managed this without bumping into each other although our Scout Master took bigger steps and got a bit ahead of the rest of the troop.

Being a Scout was a good experience for all of us. From the Scouts we learnt to be good citizens, self-reliant, honest, helpful to others and to "Be prepared". This cost us our subscription of 3d per week, some food from the larder for camping, and the occasional bus fare.

With Lord and Lady Baden-Powell as her parents, it was only natural that Betty Clay should find herself involved with Guides and Scouts throughout her life:

In 1942-3 my husband Gervas and I were living at Isoka, a district in the northern part of Northern Rhodesia (now Zambia) bordering on Tanganyika (Tanzania) and Nyasaland (Malawi). We went to Abercorn to visit the dentist (about 150 miles!) and there was a camp set up there for some of the Polish refugees; they had fled from Poland and travelled via the Middle East and East Africa till at last they found a temporary home there. Someone told us there might be some Scouts and Guides among them, so we went to see. It was not easy to make ourselves understood, but I wore a Guide badge and did the Salute. I used all the languages I knew for the name "Scout" and "Guide", but they still looked mystified until suddenly

Gervas said "Baden-Powell?", to which there was a miraculous response. Their faces lit up, they repeated the name, they shouted to their friends, they ran and fetched several people who came running; grinning all over their faces they rushed to shake our hands with the left hand, and at last found an interpreter. It was wonderful to feel that here, in the depths of Africa and in all their depression and anxiety, we were able to bring them the comfort and the joy of being part of this great world brother-and sisterhood of Scouting and Guiding.

In 1946 Gervas was transferred to Kitwe, the township for the Nkana Copper Mine, so for the first time we lived in a town and had to learn a very different lifestyle from that of our previous ten years of bush-life. During those years, I had had no opportunity to be active in the Guide Movement, but this was now quickly remedied: I was asked if I would take on the local European Guide Company, as their Guider was leaving. When I demurred that I "couldn't possibly, never done it, don't know anything", the cheery Patrol Leaders said "Don't worry, we'll teach you." This they did to such good effect that they won a national competition the following year. They then started a Ranger Company, in which they promoted me from captain to major. As other people have found, "once a Guide always a Guide".

The Royal visit in 1947 was a very special occasion. Their Majesties King George VI and Queen Elizabeth, accompanied by Princess Elizabeth and Princess Margaret, toured South Africa and Southern Rhodesia and spent a few days at Livingstone, near the Victoria Falls. One day was allocated to official functions, to which people came from all over Northern Rhodesia. There were special trains from the Copperbelt, one of them for Scouts and Guides, on which I was one of the escorts for the 24-hour journey. It was quite a job to keep an eye on these excited children, as they raced up and down that long train, but it was a relief to know that as Scouts and Guides they could be trusted.

At Livingstone there was a "rehearsal" of the parade, and people were allocated their places. You can imagine the unbelievable thrill we all had when Their Majesties arrived; I don't think we have ever sung the National Anthem with such fervour as we did then, singing it actually *to* them (if we could sing at all for the lump in our throats). They walked along the lines of their loyal subjects, shaking hands with and talking to many — of whom I was honoured to be one — and I'm sure that for those Scouts and Guides their Promise "to do their duty to the King" really came alive as they saluted him in person.

We were on leave in England during 1948 and I went as a Helper to a camp for handicapped Guides at a lovely place, Woodlarks, near Farnham, Surrey, which had been adapted by its beneficent owners for such a purpose. Most of the campers were older than "Guide-age", and two or three of them were Guiders in spite of their handicaps. One bright spark, completely paralysed from the neck down, ran a very active Brownie pack from her wheel-bed. With the aid of mirrors she could see what they were doing in all directions!

I was allotted to Priscilla, a sweet young woman who bore with great courage and dignity the difficulties of cerebral palsy. Although she was mostly in her wheelchair, she could walk with help, and I admired enormously her gallant efforts to make her recalcitrant limbs do the simplest chores. She was able to talk, slowly and carefully, and we had long heart-searching and heart-rending chats as we worked together on our bits of the teamwork which enlivens and animates every camp. "Mutual help" was visible everywhere; the deaf ones pushed the wheelchairs, the wheelchair-bound did writing and sewing for the blind. The artistic ones made cards and decorations for the not-so-skilled, so that everyone had the satisfaction of achieving something worthwhile.

I remained friends with Priscilla for the rest of her life: a friendship I valued highly.

In the early stages of the war various voluntary organisations, including Scouts and Guides, met together to plan relief work for the aftermath of the war. This resolve led to the call for volunteers to look ahead and accept training in the midst of their current war work. Betty Bindloss, who had been involved in the Guide Movement for many years, volunteered with enthusiasm:

"Training" could be done only during brief breaks, and mostly meant trying to develop our physical and mental capacity so that we could deal as best we could in unforeseen circumstances. I learnt how to skin and paunch a rabbit and how to drive a tractor. This latter exploit nearly ended in disaster as no one had told me where the brake was. I found it at the last moment.

Each volunteer had to undergo a short weekend containing unexpected physical emergencies. Mine was spent in the Pennines, with about six others, pulling a trek-cart full of equipment several miles over rough country, taking it to pieces to get it over stone walls, then reassembling it with its load. We had no food or drink all day (we sucked pebbles!), and spent a night out in the heather under the stars. Then we had to get ourselves back to work before the end of a 72-hour leave. I had to get from the Pennines to Ely, Cambridgeshire.

By early 1945 it was possible for relief teams to begin their work in Europe, and a Mobile Hospital of 50 beds, completely self-sufficient and stocked with all necessary equipment, was prepared for our Guide group. In addition, provision had to be made for cooking and caring not only for the patients but also for a team of nurses, doctors, drivers, laboratory pathologists and assistants. We set sail for Belgium with our ambulances, lorries and jeeps in a Tank Landing Craft on 24 February 1945.

This was the beginning of a year packed with experiences — a challenging year when over and over again I was eternally grateful for Guide training in "Be preparedness" — not only of the physical sort but being prepared to live in crowded conditions among strangers. At times we were bored and frustrated, at others fearfully overworked. I learnt to make myself reasonably comfortable in every type of living condition, being prepared for danger and dirt, for despair and delight.

When we reached Holland, only half the country had been freed; its people were exhausted and hungry. We found ourselves first setting up a makeshift hospital in the grounds of a boys' school in a monastery. We slept in monastic cells where every night the windows fell open with the bang of a gun some miles away, shooting down German rockets on their way to England. We were sent all over the place to cope with different situations, generally following up the Army, supposedly to help with civilian casualties.

Sometimes we drove our vehicles to transport refugees or workers. Often we were on the heels of the retreating German Army, billeted in places they had just left, and we spent more time on our knees with scrapers and scrubbing brushes than in ministering to the sick, until we landed up in a Dutch town on the River Waal where a typhoid epidemic was raging. The sewers in villages the length of the river had been smashed, all the way to Rotterdam. There we spent three months, turning a large school into a hospital. To start with, there were no working lavatories, no hot water, nothing in which to soak infected bed-linen or excreta before disposal. Dutch collaborators were drafted in to deal with this problem, and gradually we got better organised as a hospital.

The next months were immensely busy and rewarding. We made friends with the townspeople and had Guide contacts there, too. Gradually the epidemic was brought under control and the Dutch took over. Then we were ready to be sent into Germany, into the Harz Mountains area, right in the middle of the Displaced Labourers' Camps. These were workers from all the Eastern European countries who had been forcibly taken from their homes to work for the Germans in factories and farms, living in camps set up where the need for labourers was greatest.

We had medical wards — a TB ward and a maternity ward — with German help in the kitchen and a comfortable mess in which to relax. We had Christmas there, in a peace-filled world, an indescribable sensation for our slave-labourer patients and their families. With the help of Red Cross parcels we were able to give them presents: luxuries like soap, toothbrushes, face-flannels, combs, hankies, and similar civilised "extras", after years of deprivation.

Elsie Dickinson spent her early years in Southport, where she joined the Brownies, then the Guides, and finally the Sea Rangers:

The uniform I wore when I joined the 29th Southport St Philip's Guide Company was very different from that worn today. We wore a knee-length blue cotton tunic, with a leather belt that had the Guide emblem, the trefoil, on the buckle. I slid a leather purse on to my belt and also carried a Guide knife with a marline spike attached on one side and whistle on the other.

The tunic had two breast pockets. On one of these I stitched a vertical white stripe when I was promoted from the Kingfisher Patrol to Seconder in the Bluetits. Later, when I became Patrol Leader, I had two stripes plus a lanyard. Our company wore green ties that could be used as triangular bandages if necessary — so useful for First Aid. Each company wore a different colour.

We also wore a navy-blue felt hat with quite a wide brim. These had the unfortunate habit of shrinking in the rain. Our captain and lieutenant wore a better-quality hat, turned up on one side with a cockade. They wore a navy suit over a blue blouse.

The company was divided into four patrols, each called after a bird. The leaders occasionally took turns to be in charge and organise an evening's activities. We always had a session in our patrols studying some aspect of Guiding, maybe helping a Tenderfoot to learn the "promise", or tie knots. We had a parade to check whether we had polished our badges and shoes, and were generally well presented. We each brought a penny for funds, which were collected after the inspection.

Later we would play a game like "Twos and Threes" indoors; in summer, rounders in the playground of the school where we met was popular. Sometimes we had a treasure-hunt or went tracking in the near vicinity. We usually had a period in which we could exchange library books: these were kept in a large, musty suitcase in the cycle shed.

Our captain took a group to camp each summer, usually to Waddington, near Clitheroe, but I had no desire to sleep under canvas at that stage. I was, however, keen to work for badges and soon earned my Second Class badge, plus First Aider and others. I almost won my First Class badge, but I could never have managed the swimming — I was terrified of water for a long time.

During the war a brand new Sea Ranger Company was formed, the only one in Southport, by an ex-WREN, and I was glad to join it.

We were very proud of our new uniform — navy skirt with white blouse and black triangular tie, held in place with a woggle. We also had a white lanyard and whistle.

There was a navy beret with a badge, similar to the Guide badge but enamelled blue, at one side.

We were to study sailing with the Sea Scouts. By then I could swim one length, but it needed a very determined effort for me to swim the two lengths required before they would risk taking us on the Marine Lake. Sailing to me was a cold, wet job. My beret was knocked off into the water on the only occasion I went, so I was not exactly smitten with the sailing bug.

Now I was sufficiently confident to leave home, and joined the others as we camped at Wray Castle, between Ambleside and Hawkshead. I thoroughly enjoyed the experience despite pouring rain the day we arrived. We were compelled to sleep on the hard floor in the nearby schoolroom. After a couple of days with the tents up, the ground had dried sufficiently and those who wished were allowed to sleep outside. I delighted in the smell of fresh grass at dawn, as we always slept with the brailling rolled up.

We had to be highly organised and shipshape every morning for inspection. Each "watch", or patrol, took it in turn to cook for those going out for the day. Cooking porridge in a hay-box overnight was quite magical to me.

We walked miles each day, and sang as we walked, teaching each other new Guide songs, which seemed to make the distance shorter.

William (Bill) Findlay was brought up in the Glasgow area, where the Boys' Brigade originated:

I was not quite five years old when the war began.

Uniforms appeared everywhere. One uniform which was to be denied to me, however, was school uniform. In those days uniform at a working-class village primary school was virtually unheard of, but I soon became aware of two other uniforms: those of the Scouts and the Boys' Brigade.

The Boys' Brigade was founded in 1883 by Sir William Alexander Smith, who started the movement in Glasgow. It is not a military organisation but sets great store on discipline. During the First World War there was an Army battalion comprised entirely of former BB boys and officers, known as the Boys' Brigade Battalion of the Highland Light Infantry. While nothing like this took place during the Second World War, the training given by the BB was considered suitable for young men who were likely to be called up.

Even as a five-year-old I assumed that I would be a soldier some day. As I grew up, I thought about joining something. Two older neighbours were in the BB. They liked it, and persuaded my friends to join with me when I was eight years old. In fact, I joined the reserve movement, or the Life Boys as they were then known. I remained with them until I transferred into the Boys' Brigade at the age of 12.

My Life Boy years were happy ones, despite the war. Both BB and Life Boys are Christian organisations, a fact demonstrated clearly by the people who ran them. The leader in charge of our Life Boy team didn't last long. She was called up for military service. Her colleague, an engineer, soon left for the Merchant Navy. Another leader had already left for military service before I joined. With all the staff departing, my Life Boy days might well have come to a premature end but for a remarkable woman, the mother of our original leader.

Mrs Younger, assisted by her second daughter, who was in her early teens, took over and did an outstanding job for the remainder of the war. A middle-aged lady, she had no experience of young people other than her own family. She listened to us and tried to please us but, always, she was in charge. Any challenge to her authority would be greeted by "I'll just have a word with your mother about your behaviour" — and it worked.

The black-out made it unsafe for us to meet in the evening, so our Life Boy team met on a Saturday afternoon for a while. Later, however, we reverted to an evening meeting. Being a Life Boy was great fun, but we all admired the older boys who were in the Boys' Brigade. Our company ran three football teams. The senior team won the Glasgow Battalion Championship the year before I was due to join it, and several of the boys went on to become professional footballers.

The company also had a pipe band, run mainly by three brothers, the Hardies, one of whom became a world piping champion. With such talent, it is hardly surprising that the company band also won the Glasgow Battalion Championship. This was during the same year as the football title.

As Life Boys, we shared in the glory achieved by the BB Company to which we belonged, the 268th Glasgow. We were also proud of the attainments of ex-members of other Glasgow companies who became war heroes. Flying Officer Drew McPherson, an officer in the 32nd Glasgow Boys' Brigade, was the first person to receive the DFC during the war; and Sergeant John Hannah, ex-member of the 237th Glasgow, was the first Scot to be awarded the VC. John Hannah was only 18 when he won that award.

The war was over by the time I moved from the Life Boys to the Boys' Brigade. One of the first things that a BB boy has to learn is the object of the movement. "The object of the Boys' Brigade is the advancement of Christ's Kingdom among boys, and the promotion of habits of obedience, reverence, discipline, self-respect, and all that tends towards a true Christian manliness."

In those days obedience, reverence, discipline and self-respect were valued qualities, and being a BB boy stood one in good stead. The drill and discipline was excellent preparation for National Service. The Christian teaching I received led me into the Church, first as a member, then elder, then reader (or lay preacher as it is sometimes called).

Other things I learned in the Boys' Brigade were also of value: First Aid, for example. Other than the Christian aspect, perhaps the greatest contribution the Boys' Brigade made to society was that it taught boys the value of fellowship and how to work together for the common good.

Grace Horseman arranged a post-war reunion for *BOB* friends:

During the war BOBs were in different parts of the country, and travelling restrictions made it impossible for

271

us to meet as a group. Also, several were married with young children, but we managed to keep in touch by letter and telephone.

One of us, Marjorie Coward, was teaching English at Ashford Grammar School and rented a delightful oast house in Kent during the war. Somehow I managed to get permission to visit her and was intrigued by the large circular living-room and the ladder that led to the bedroom above. It was charming and in a beautiful situation. We had a mini-meeting on our own, sharing the songs and poems we loved, and vowed that in 1957 we would all meet at Burford Bridge Hotel, Box Hill, Surrey, on 26 February (the 57th day of the year), as we had promised ourselves years earlier. It proved to be a wonderful reunion when we stayed there for the weekend. We forgot we were now staid grown-ups as we climbed up the slippery slopes of the hill in the rain, singing and dancing. From then on we met frequently, with the same effervescent joy.

The years have passed, but those of us who are still alive keep in touch, and trust we shall one day be reunited with those with whom we have shared so much fun and happiness.

A long-forgotten verse we used to share:

> When I go free,
> I think 'twill be
> A night of stars and snow,
> And the wild fires of frost shall light
> My footsteps as I go;
> Nobody — nobody will be there
> With groping touch, or sight,

To see me in my bush of hair
Dance burning through the night.

('The Little Salamander"
by Walter de la Mare)

BIBLIOGRAPHY

Patricia Baker: *Fashions of a Decade: The 1940s* (Batsford, 1991)

Jennifer Davies: *The Wartime Kitchen Garden* (BBC Books, 1993)

Nance Lui Fyson: *Portrait of a Decade: The 1940s* (Batsford, 1988)

Norman Longman: *How We Lived Then: A History of Everyday Life during the Second World War* (Arrow Books, 1991)

Juliana Ray: *By Grace Alone* (Marshall Pickering, 1985)

Anthony Russell: *The Clerical Profession* (SPCK, 1980)

Richard Tames: *World War Two: Life in Wartime Britain* (Batsford, 1993)

Barry Turner and Tony Rennell: *When Daddy Came Home: How Family Life Changed for Ever in 1945* (Hutchinson, 1988)

Anne Valery: *Talking about the War, 1939-1940: A Personal View of War in Britain* (Michael Joseph, 1991)

Alec Vidler: *The Church in the Time of Revolution* (Pelican Church History series, 1961)

Sadie Ward: *War in the Countryside, 1939-1945* (David & Charles, 1988)

CONTRIBUTORS

Mrs Nina Armour
Chesham, Bucks

Mrs Noreen Beaumont
Southampton, Hants

Miss Betty Bindloss
Bovey Tracey, Devon

Mrs Louise Boreham
Buntisland, Fife

Mrs Peggy Brackenbury
Abergele, Clwyd

Mrs Isla Brownless
Chichester, West Sussex

The Rev P P S Brownless,
MA
Chichester, West
Sussex

Mr Edward Chaplin
Crowborough, East
Sussex

The Hon Mrs Clay
Taunton, Somerset

Miss Gillian Clay
Taunton, Somerset

Mr Gary Cornford
London

Mr Dick Cunningham,
Johannesburg, South
Africa

Mrs Anna Cunningham
Johannesburg, South
Africa

Mrs Elsie Dickinson
Knaresbrook, North
Yorks

Mr Bill Findlay
Bishopbriggs, Glasgow

Mrs Iris Harris
Shrewsbury, Shropshire

Mrs Barbara Hillier
Exeter, Devon

Mrs Grace Horseman
Bovey Tracey, Devon

Mrs Mary Horseman
Bristol, Avon

Mrs Vivienne Hubbard
Hornsea, North
Humberside

Mrs Elizabeth Hughes
Oswestry, Powys

Dr Graham Jardine
Bearsden, Glasgow

Mr E W A Knight
Totnes, Devon

Mrs Muriel Lees
Castleton, Rochdale

Mrs Doris Maguire
Naphill, Bucks

Miss Betty Matson
Benfleet, Essex

Miss Margaret McDonald
Slough, Berks

Mr John McKay
Market Harborough,
Leics

Mrs Gill Meason
Dartford, Kent

Mr George Moore
Bristol, Avon

Mr Masao Morihara
Japan

Sqn. Leader A J Mott,
MBE
Petersfield, Hants

Mr Mervyn G Mott
Bristol, Avon

Major P E Mott
Sunningdale, Berks

Mrs Joan Newall
Hertford, Herts

Mrs Ivy Page
Naphill, Bucks

276

Mrs Elsie Paget
Rochester, Kent

Mr Henry Patterson
Bishopbriggs, Glasgow

Mrs Christine Powell
Bovey Tracey, Devon

Mrs Anne Power
Bovey Tracey,
Devon

Miss Joan Preston
Plymouth, Devon

Mr Louis Quinain
Wellington, Somerset

Mrs Juliana Ray
London

Mrs Elizabeth Risius
Erpingham,
Norwich

Miss Edith Rolfe
London

Mrs Sakue Shimohore
Japan

Lt Commander Ian
Sandeman
Plymouth,
Devon

Mr Keith Spooner
Liskeard, Cornwall

Mr Dennis E Thompson
Aylesbury, Bucks

Mr H Jim West
Deal, Kent

Col (retired) John R West,
MBE
Chichester, West
Sussex

ISIS publish a wide range of books in large
print, from fiction to biography. A full list of
titles is available free of charge from the
address below. Alternatively, contact your
local library for details of their collection of
ISIS large print books.

Details of ISIS complete and unabridged
audio books are also available.

Any suggestions for books you would like to
see in large print or audio are always
welcome.

ISIS

7 Centremead
Osney Mead
Oxford OX2 0ES
(01865) 250333